Brimming with creative inspiration, how-to projects, and useful information to enrich your everyday life, Quarto Knows is a favorite destination for those pursuing their interests and passions. Visit our site and dig deeper with our books into your area of interest: Quarto Creates, Quarto Cooks, Quarto Homes, Quarto Lives, Quarto Drives, Quarto Explores, Quarto Gifts, or Quarto Kids.

First published in 2018 by Motorbooks, an imprint of The Quarto Group, 401 Second Avenue North, Suite 310, Minneapolis, MN 55401 USA. T (612) 344-8100 F (612) 344-8692 www.QuartoKnows.com

Motorbooks titles are also available at discount for retail, wholesale, promotional, and bulk purchase. For details, contact the Special Sales Manager by email at specialsales@quarto.com or by mail at The Quarto Group, Attn: Special Sales Manager, 401 Second Avenue North, Suite 310, Minneapolis, MN 55401 USA.

10 9 8 7 6 5 4 3 2 1

ISBN: 978-0-7603-6303-4

Library of Congress Cataloging-in-Publication Data

Cotter, Tom, 1954- author.
   Tom Cotter's best barn-find collector car tales / Tom Cotter.
Other titles: Best barn-find collector car tales
Description: Minneapolis, MN, USA : Motorbooks, 2018. | Includes index.
Identifiers: LCCN 2018018913 | ISBN 9780760363034
LCSH: Automobiles--Collectors and collecting. | Antique and classic cars--Anecdotes.
LCC TL7.A1 C6845 2018 | DDC 629.222075--dc23

Acquiring Editor: Zack Miller
Project Manager: Nyle Vialet
Art Director: Brad Springer
Cover Designer: Simon Larkin
Interior Design: Emily Weigel
Layout: John Sticha

On the front cover: A vintage truck is revealed behind a forgotten garage door. *iStock/bluebeat76*

On the back cover: Winnebago or Windsor? Chrome meets rust on this aging emblem. *Michael Alan Ross*

On the endpapers: A Cobra (front) and Buick Eight (back). *Michael Alan Ross*

On the frontis: The fin of a Caddy and the wire wheel of a Jag make for an interesting conversation starter. What else lies behind these doors? *Michael Alan Ross*

Printed in China

Tom Cotter's BEST
BARN-FIND
COLLECTOR
CAR TALES

CONTENTS

INTRODUCTION

Barn finding has become a sport over the past couple of decades. Once the exclusive activity of "junkyard men," who merely sought to fill their scrap yards with fresh "inventory," barn finding has become the hobby, and the occasional career, for adventurous old car enthusiasts. When I open a barn door, I don't know if I'll be treated to a Ferrari, a Falcon, or just a pile of hay. But it's always equally exciting and gives adults like me the opportunity to become a kid again.

There are no prerequisites or advanced degrees required to search for old cars, just a flashlight, an old set of clothes, and above-average enthusiasm. It's dirty, but it's fun. Or, like when you were a kid, perhaps it's fun because it's dirty!

Keeping your eyes open while driving through new areas, asking at auto parts stores and repair shops "Are there any old car guys around?", and following up on leads makes this more of a treasure hunt and less of a chore. There is simply no way I would rather spend a Saturday.

I'm sure I didn't invent barn finding, but I've sure been at it for a

long time. When I wrote *The Cobra in the Barn*, nearly twenty years ago, there were no TV shows like *American Pickers*, *Chasing Classic Cars*, or any of the multitude of variations currently seen on The History Channel, Velocity, and others. But I'm sure my book opened the eyes of old car enthusiasts to this previously underground activity. This is now my tenth book on the subject.

When Hagerty Insurance and Shell Oil approached me a few years ago about hosting a YouTube program on the subject, I only asked that it be authentic and that I didn't need to bring urgency, anger, and false drama to the subject. The result is *Barn Find Hunter*, and it's still going strong several years in. And true to their word, when you watch that program, it's really me.

This "Best of" book is a collection of my favorite barn find stories I've collected, written about, or heard over the past couple of decades. There is a Cobra story here and there but plenty of blue-collar cars as well because I've found out that the true value of barn finding has nothing to do with the cost of the car, but everything to do with the story.

So roll up your sleeves and dive in. But bring a flashlight and wear old clothes, because it's dirty out there. Let me know what you find.

Happy hunting!

TWO-WHEELED WONDERS

THE JURASSIC
JUNKYARD

Al Kelly is a self-described crapoholic. He likes nothing more than to buy, sell, or barter parts for his vintage motorcycle or car restoration projects. In the 1980s, the tool and die maker spotted some old cars and parts behind the Mount Hope Texaco, which was about a thirty-minute drive from his home in Branchville, New Jersey. When he spotted the parts, he pulled over his freshly restored 1948 GMC pickup and stopped in to check it out.

"I asked the owner if anything in the junkyard was for sale," Kelly said. "He cursed me out and told me to mind my own business and never come back." He didn't go back for almost twenty years.

One day he was at his job when he received a call in the late afternoon. The caller told Kelly that the eccentric junkyard owner had suffered a stroke, and the town was demanding that the family clean up the property immediately.

"Apparently, he had grown up in the same town and was a bit of an oddball," Kelly said. "He would save every piece of metal he could find—every scrap, every bottle cap. He believed that if there were another world war, he would become rich from recycling all his metal. All this metal was mounded up in sloppy piles, and you had to make your way through on these small paths between the garbage.

"The town actually jailed him once because he refused to clean up his property."

Kelly knew the old man had also been a motorcycle enthusiast in his younger days. When the call came in at 11:30 a.m., he got up from his desk and simply walked out of the factory without saying anything to anyone.

Al Kelly and his brother Ken are lifelong crapoholics. Ken stands in front of the hole they smashed in the side of a storage building in Mount Hope, New Jersey. It was the only way they could drag out the motorcycle treasure hidden inside. *Ken Kelly*

"I was so excited," he said.

When Kelly arrived at Mount Hope Texaco, he was greeted by the old man's twenty-something nephew, Dave.

"I asked if I could look at some of the motorcycles and parts and he said, 'Yeah, sure, go ahead,'" Kelly said.

Kelly came across piles of junk, which reminded him of a scene from the movie *Jurassic Park*. At least fifty old cars were scattered about. The cars were models from between the 1920s and the 1950s. He also found piles of motorcycle parts mixed in with the automotive hulks and scraps.

"Apparently, he had some trouble with guys sneaking in and stealing motorcycles and parts," he said, "so he took the bikes partially apart and hid them around the junkyard."

Then Kelly saw something that shocked him and made him realize that time was of the essence.

"There was a crusher in the middle of the yard, and it was about to come down on a 1920s Indian," he said. "I was yelling at the crusher operator to stop, and he was yelling at me to get back."

Inside the shed that had no doors were a number of bikes, including a 1957 Harley, a 1944 military Indian, and this 1930 Indian Scout. The Kelly brothers bought all three bikes for $450 each. *Ken Kelly*

The Indian was lost, but Kelly realized that if they were crushing Indian motorcycles for the value of scrap, he should be able to buy things real cheap.

"There were other scavengers in the yard looking for gold, so I knew I had to work quickly," Kelly said. "I saw an old bike leaning against a shed, and it was surrounded by a bunch of old parts. It was about [a] twenty-four-by-thirty-foot building, but there was so much crap piled against it that I couldn't find the way in.

"I just crawled through some old auto parts until I found a hole in the wall and I crawled in. The place was ready to fall down. It was so dark in there that I really couldn't see, but I put out my hands and felt motorcycles in that building.

"So I covered my tracks, sealed up the hole in the wall, and left to get my brother Ken, who was also into old bikes."

Before he left, Kelly had accumulated some smaller parts he was interested in—motorcycle seats and vintage motorcycle license plates—and asked Dave if he would take $25 for the parts, all the money in his wallet.

"Sure," said Dave.

Then Kelly said, "Oh, wait, this is all the money I have. Can I give you just twenty dollars so I have five dollars for lunch?" Dave agreed, and Kelly sped off to pick up his brother from work.

"Ken, listen, you've got to come with me right now," he said. "Don't tell anyone; just jump in because everything in that junkyard is selling fast.

"You got to see this."

Kelly drove fast and made it back in forty minutes, record time for the roundtrip.

The two Kellys went right back to the barn and climbed back inside. The brothers couldn't see a thing, but they were able to feel a spring front end on one of the bikes, so they knew it was an Indian. They also felt a couple of other bikes but couldn't identify the brands in the dark.

"We climbed back out and asked Dave how much he wanted for each motorcycle," he said.

"I'll take three hundred dollars each."

So the brothers dragged out their three-bike stash through a larger hole they ripped in the side of the shed wall. The bikes included the Indian, actually a 1930 101 Scout; a 1957 Harley-Davidson Hummer; and a 1944 Indian Military Scout.

"Hey, you weren't supposed to go in there," barked Dave, reminding Kelly of the similar angry tone his uncle had barked twenty years earlier.

"I can't sell those beauties for three hundred dollars," he said, even though he never even knew there were bikes in the shed. "I'll need at least four hundred fifty dollars each for those bikes."

"Deal," said the two Kellys.

In addition to the three motorcycles, the Kellys also dragged out a complete 1946 Harley Knucklehead engine in good condition and some skirted Indian fenders.

The Kellys sold off the 1944 Indian Military Scout and the 1957 Harley, but to this day, they retain the 1930 Indian.

"Finding these bikes wasn't the only treasure—restoring and riding them is also a treasure," Al Kelly said.

A crapoholic's dream come true.

YOU'RE ONLY CRAZY ONCE

"Wear your oldest clothes," Dick Fritz said to his colleagues. "And don't forget the Liquid Wrench."

Fritz and his friends Rich and Ben were packing for a trip overseas. Usually, old clothes and Liquid Wrench would never make it onto even the most casual tourist's packing list. But these three were about to embark on the barn-find adventure of a lifetime. In just a few hours, the trio would be on a Delta Airlines flight from New York's John F. Kennedy Airport to the most unlikely destination of Sheremetyevo International Airport in Moscow, Russia.

They were on the hunt for the elusive armor-plated Mercedes 540K Aktion P. Fritz had been a car guy his whole life. His first car was a 1939 Ford convertible that he purchased for $125 from a neighbor in 1956. His father warned him, "I wouldn't buy that car if I were you!" But Fritz did what teenaged boys are supposed to do, and he bought it anyway, explaining to his dad, "But you're not me . . ."

It was in sad condition, with a ripped top and torn upholstery. But the money saved from mowing lawns enabled him to purchase a new top and install seat covers. Eventually he painted the car—using a small compressor he had used to paint model airplanes—and installed a 1953 Mercury V-8 with two carburetors and dual exhaust.

Eventually that car was sold, and a succession of Chevrolets followed, including a 1955 Chevy and a new 1963 fuel-injected Corvette.

Yet it was motorcycles that left the first motor vehicle impression on young Fritz, who at six years old was already witnessing motorcycle circus tricks in his backyard.

"I grew up in a neighborhood near Nyack, New York, and behind us lived a real clown who had traveled with circuses around the world," said Fritz. "He would have fellow circus performers visit, one of which would arrive pulling a travel trailer, and inside was a motorcycle which he used in his act.

"Even though my father would have killed him [if he knew], he would take me for rides when my father was at work."

As he got older, both cars and motorcycles took a back seat to education for Fritz. His intention was to pursue a degree in aeronautical engineering, but when the car bug bit, he changed his major to mechanical engineering and enrolled in the engineering program at Clarkston University in New York.

Enrolled in the same college was the son of a respected auto racing personality, Luigi Chinetti. Chinetti had been a champion race driver in Europe—having won the 24 Hours of Le Mans three times—before emigrating to the United States in 1940. Chinetti later became Ferrari's first North American importer. Chinetti's son, Luigi Jr., would invite Fritz to work on the racing team's pit crew at tracks such as Watkins Glen, Lime Rock, and Sebring. "Soon after I graduated from college in 1962, I was called by Mr. Chinetti to come to work at the dealership," Fritz said. "I was twenty-two—what did I know? But Mr. Chinetti said they needed a manager, so I took the job."

He remained there until 1978.

"I handled the importation, sold Ferraris, managed the Ferrari North American Racing Team, designed race car components, handled customer service, designed and installed the first automatic transmission in a Ferrari along with the first Ferrari air pollution control systems, and basically was involved in the whole business," he said.

The Ferrari business wasn't always as robust as the company has been in recent years. There were times, according to Fritz, when the company couldn't make payroll for its small office staff and mechanics.

"With Mr. Chinetti's permission, I opened up a company called Amerispec in 1976," he said. Amerispec was a company that specialized in the legalization of imported cars for use on US roads. "The US Ferrari business wasn't really good in 1975. All they imported to us was the eight-cylinder Dino 308 GT4 model, which not too many people seemed to want, so we legalized the twelve-cylinder Boxer Berlinettas and 400 Automatics.

"Mr. Chinetti was seventy-five years old and wanted to sell the business, but I knew I didn't want to work for whomever bought it, so I worked nights and weekends developing my own business in the meantime."

In time, Amerispec thrived as it federalized such cars as the Ferrari Boxer, the Porsche 959, and the McLaren F1 during the boom days of the 1980s.

His customers included Jay Leno, Ralph Lauren, and David Letterman. Then it all went bust as Amerispec tried to tread water during the economic downturn of the early 1990s.

Then one day the phone rang. "Hello," the caller said to Fritz. "Can you help me get my two cars I've imported from Russia out of a container and into this country legally?" Fritz was curious and asked the gentleman, who was obviously also from Russia, "What kind of cars are they?"

"A Mercedes and a Horch, which I hope to sell over here," the gentleman said. He continued, saying there were lots of valuable German cars in Russia to be found.

A light bulb went off in Fritz's head.

"There wasn't much exotic car business going on in 1992 with the recession and all," he said. "So instead of just sitting around the office waiting for the phone to ring, I thought it might be a profitable adventure."

He quickly called his friend Rich Reuter, whose family had owned a restoration business for three generations.

"Because they had restored so many Mercedes-Benzes, I thought of Rich first because he was an expert on the vintage models," Fritz said.

"And it just so happened that Rich had a friend in Moscow who was a writer and a literary guy who could possibly help us out. Then I mentioned it to a customer, Ben, who was instantly interested and said he would be willing to back us financially if we included him."

Suddenly it was a "go," and the three men were packing for a trip to Russia. Because they didn't want to stand out from the Russian population, they decided to wear old clothes and bring containers of Liquid Wrench in case they needed to remove rusty bolts from any of the cars they were hoping to find. Reuter knew just one Russian, but word soon began to spread even before they landed that three American car enthusiasts were coming to Russia in search of old cars. In addition, "agents" from Tennessee said they would be glad to show them rare Russian car collections that could be purchased once they landed.

"We brought over thirty thousand or forty thousand dollars in American cash, each of us taking a third of the pile of one-hundred-dollar bills," Fritz said.

"We carried the cash in our jackets just in case they searched our checked luggage, which they never did. If they had, a less-than-honest customs agent might call his friends on the outside and you'd never be seen again.

"I must admit, though, that carrying around forty thousand dollars in cash was frightening, knowing that at the time tourists were being killed in Russia for as little as two hundred dollars."

When they arrived in Moscow, they checked into a very nice hotel, which was owned by Lufthansa Airlines. It felt somewhat out of place at the very time when the economy of the Soviet Union was collapsing. The plan was to meet their Tennessee connections in the hotel lobby the next morning at 10 a.m.

By 11:30 a.m., they had not shown up.

So as Fritz, Reuter, and Ben waited and waited, an interpreter they had hired mentioned that he knew of a motorcycle collector nearby who might be interested in selling some bikes.

"Well, we weren't doing anything there in the hotel, so I said I would go look at them because the other two guys didn't know anything about motorcycles, and at least I knew a little," Fritz said.

Fritz and his interpreter drove across Moscow into an area crowded with apartment complexes. He was then asked by a young man to crawl through a four-foot-tall window down under the sidewalk and into a dark basement. He didn't know if he would ever come out again.

He entered the six-foot-tall basement, and it took a few minutes before his eyes could adjust to the dim light.

"The bikes he had down there were really neat," Fritz said. "There was a military Indian Model 741, which wasn't in very good shape. Then there was a military Harley-Davidson WLA 42, a Matchless, and a BMW R35. He also had several Russian motorcycles, but I wasn't really interested in those because there was really no market for them in the States."

Prior to the trip, Fritz had done some research about American motorcycles in Russia and discovered that the United States had given a couple of thousand Harleys and Indians to the Soviet government during World War II to assist in fighting the Nazi army. These bikes had been built to US Army specifications but were basically street models that had some different details and were painted Olive Drab.

"I have no idea how he ever got the bikes down here, through that small opening next to the sidewalk," he said. "The owner was a young guy, probably between twenty-five and twenty-eight years old. He was clean cut, good-looking, and calm. At this point in our trip, I didn't know who I could

Dick Fritz tired of waiting for his classic car contacts in the Moscow hotel, so he left his two colleagues and pursued the rumor of some classic old motorcycles rusting away in the area. When he arrived at this apartment house, he was told to crawl down into the basement access door under the window. *Dick Fritz*

trust and who I couldn't trust, but dealing with this guy, I got the feeling that I could trust him."

Without consulting his colleagues, Fritz decided to buy the bikes if they could be had for a fair price.

"I would never come up with a price first," he said. "I would always let the seller come up with a price and then say, 'That's way too much money.'

"Over time, we realized that many of the Russians would start by asking twenty thousand dollars for a bike or car. When I'd tell them that was too much money, they'd say, 'OK, then how about two thousand.' We'd sometimes be able to negotiate down to three hundred and fifty dollars."

Fritz's negotiation with the young fellow was much easier than most others they would experience, though. He paid about $200 for each bike, so he felt pretty good about his $800 investment when he joined his two colleagues back in the hotel lobby a little while later, still waiting for their Tennessee brokers.

"Hey, I think I just bought enough motorcycles to pay for our trip," he said. "I bought four of them."

Reuter was fine with the purchase, but the financier, Ben, was skeptical.

"You bought motorcycles?" he asked. "What did you do that for?"

"I told him not to worry, we'd make money with them," Fritz said. "I figured they had to be worth at least ten thousand dollars, which would put this trip in the black."

Fritz had arranged with the bikes' owner to store them until shipping arrangements could be secured.

Their Tennessee brokers finally showed up the next morning, twenty-four hours after the appointed time. They led their fellow Yankees to a muddy, dirty field where a number of steel shipping containers were located that people used as garages. The steel doors had three locks on them so that the contents could not be stolen.

"They told us about this very rare four-wheel-drive Mercedes-Benz touring car that had been specially built for a Nazi field marshal," Fritz said. "It was something like a 1937 or '38 230 Mercedes.

"I looked at it and said to Rich, 'This is junk.' He said, 'I know.' It was the body of a Mercedes mounted onto the chassis, suspension, and drivetrain from some sort of Soviet military truck. And he was trying to tell us that it was all original."

"We didn't want to say anything negative to this guy because who knows if he might turn up something worthwhile in the future."

The Tennessee brokers said they had an option to buy a rare Mercedes 770K and a Horch, but they were nine hundred miles away, and they needed to sell this Mercedes 4x4 before they could buy those cars. They also showed them photos of a Mercedes 500K and a Horch, which they said they had just sold and were on their way to America, which Fritz studied carefully. He noticed a little red-and-blue sticker under the hood of the Horch and wondered what it might be for.

In the basement, Fritz was shown this 1935 Matchless, along with an assortment of frames, engines, and other parts. Fritz guesses the owner, Victor Litvak, was in his mid-twenties. *Dick Fritz*

Fritz and his colleagues said they would be in touch and went searching for other cars in the Moscow area.

Their interpreter on this trip, Stash, was a sharp fellow, and he kept asking people throughout Moscow if they knew of any old cars that were for sale.

"We had seen so many cars, but most of them were junk," Fritz said. "Many had some sort of Russian engines adapted into them, were undesirable models, or were in such terrible condition that it didn't make any sense to ship them halfway around the world.

"But the motorcycles kept showing up."

Finally, after they had spent a week in Russia, they were preparing to go home, empty-handed except for the four vintage motorcycles they had secured on the first day they arrived. But clearly, it was rare old cars that would command a small fortune back home that they were after.

Then, at 10 p.m. the night before they had planned to leave, they got a call from Stash. He told them of a friend of his who had a bunch of valuable cars.

"OK, let's go," Fritz said.

So they drove to the outskirts of Moscow and met an interesting, neat older fellow who sported a full beard.

"He was apparently a famous artist in Russia. We talked with him for quite a while, then he invited us to see his cars and motorcycles he had in the barn," Fritz said.

"He had quite a few interesting cars and bikes, including a familiar Mercedes 540K and Horch. When he opened the Horch hood to show us the engine, I saw that red-and-blue sticker that I had seen in those photos from the Tennessee guys. I said to Rich, 'Those cars belong to this guy!' Reuter replied, 'I know.'"

The artist said he enjoyed inviting people to tour his collection and take photos, but he wasn't interested in selling any of them. That's when they realized their Tennessee friends were in fact con artists.

So Fritz, Reuter, and Ben returned home without having purchased any ultra-rare classics but secure in their purchase of the four vintage motorcycles.

"We went home without finding any real treasures, but we knew we'd be going back again soon," Fritz said.

A few weeks later, Reuter got word from a friend that a Swede named Peter had contacted her and said he had found an armor-plated Mercedes 540K in Estonia that was for sale. That's all Fritz, Reuter, and Ben needed to hear; they made reservations and flew back to Moscow as soon as they could.

Once in Moscow, they boarded a train for the eleven-hour trip to Saint Petersburg, then another eleven-hour trip to the former Soviet territory of

Estonia. They rode in the second-class section so they wouldn't stand out as wealthy Americans.

Once in their four-berth sleeping unit, Fritz took a metal clothes hanger he had packed to wire the two door levers shut from the inside so they couldn't be robbed while they slept.

Peter the Swede, a forty-something-year-old adventure-seeker who sported a ponytail and specialized in finding World War II vintage aircraft, met them at the train station. Because he was essentially a scavenger of old things, he said he would occasionally come upon cars and motorcycles as well. Peter, who had once spent prison time in Morocco, was very streetwise, according to Fritz, and had once worked for former race driver Bob Grossman's classic car shop in Southampton, New York.

Fritz purchased this BMW R35 from a movie studio near Saint Petersburg. He believes this is a 1936 model. The price was $1,200. *Dick Fritz*

Peter picked up the Americans at the train station with his 1979 Chevy Nova, making Fritz and his companions a little more comfortable in the foreign land. He informed his passengers that through his friends in the Old Car Club of Estonia, he had arranged for an afternoon visit to a man with an armor-plated Mercedes-Benz called the Aktion P. Fritz had done research on the Aktion P cars, mostly through an excellent story that had appeared in Volume 28, Issue 1 of *Automobile Quarterly*, and discovered that the heavy-gauge steel plate used inside lightweight aluminum bodywork and the 1 1/2-inch-thick windshield and side glass made the car virtually bulletproof. The aluminum body, in addition to keeping the overall weight of the car lighter than a steel body, also prevented magnetic bombs from being planted on it, which was apparently a popular assassination technique at the time. The car also was built sans running boards to keep unwanted passengers from hitching a ride and threatening occupants. A total of twenty Aktion Ps were built in 1943 and used by Hitler and his top officials.

Of the twenty Aktion P armored cars produced, only one was known to exist; that lone survivor sat in a museum in Prague. The rest were reputedly destroyed by angry mobs after the war ended because they symbolized Nazi aggression. At 4 p.m., Peter drove the Americans to a small farm outside of the city of Tallinn, the largest in Estonia. They looked inside the barn, which was beginning to fall in on itself, and saw piles of "stuff."

"There were old car parts, bicycles, all sorts of metal parts, just seven-foot-high unorganized piles of junk," Fritz said. "You couldn't even walk into the barn without climbing on the piles."

"There's no car in there," Reuter said.

There was a rope hanging from the rafters that Peter the Swede used to swing himself to the back of the barn, and he began looking around. "Is there a car back there?" asked Reuter.

"Well, there are pieces of a car," answered Peter.

The aluminum body was here, the chassis was leaning against the wall over there, the fenders over there. Peter used a flashlight to read the chassis numbers to the Americans: "408377." This particular car had been assigned to the motorpool at the Third Reich Chancellery in Berlin, so it had been used by Adolf Hitler, Eva Braun, and virtually all the other Nazi high officials and generals. Fritz and his colleagues had to control their enthusiasm, not wanting the car's owner to see their delight. Reuter later said that it was like winning the lottery. They had just discovered the only other surviving Aktion P.

The owner confirmed that other major components—the engine, rear axle, doors, and so on—were in five other barns in the area. The car was complete when he bought it many years earlier. He explained he had dismantled the car when his teenage daughter was very young because the KGB spy organization, the Estonian Old Car Club, and various other groups knew of the car and wanted it. At one point, the Russian Mafia had threatened to disfigure his young daughter if he didn't present them with the car. By taking it apart, he simply told those interested parties that he had sold it.

"He said he wanted something unique, and that's why he bought it," Fritz said. "He collected lots of things, including a vintage Cleveland motorcycle.

"He asked if we could stop by our local Cleveland dealership when we returned home and buy a repair manual and some parts for him. I had to explain that the original Cleveland company had been out of business for many years."

After they had dug out many of the parts, the three Americans huddled in the Nova to discuss their next move. "We wanted it," Fritz said. "We were prepared to pay fifty thousand, one hundred thousand, two hundred thousand dollars, whatever it took to own that car."

They sent their translator to the car's owner to ask how much he wanted for the car. When the translator returned, they couldn't believe their ears; he wasn't interested in selling it!

"We said, 'What?'" said Fritz.

Not wanting to waste any more time, the Americans bid farewell and continued to follow up on other cars and motorcycles in the Estonian countryside.

"We looked at some Maybachs, great big sedans, but they were missing too many parts or were too badly deteriorated," Fritz said. "One rare custom-bodied Maybach we saw had been cut up into two-foot-by-two-foot pieces and stored in an eight-foot-by-eight-foot shed. It was a rare car, but you could never restore a car that was destroyed that badly."

They returned to Tallinn and tried for several days to buy the Aktion P. Having no success, they flew home with no valuable cars but had purchased four more motorcycles, leaving Peter and his two Estonian friends to try to pry the Aktion P from its owner.

After many phone calls to Peter, they learned that maybe if they returned to Estonia, they could buy the Mercedes. They first flew to Moscow and pursued several motorcycle leads. One address was on the fifth floor of an Estonian apartment complex. They walked into the young man's small apartment to see his Harley-Davidson WLA 42 in the living room. Another partially assembled motorcycle was leaning against the wall, and wheels, tires, gas tanks, and other parts were neatly stacked on top of cabinets and along the floor.

"We took the elevator up here," Fritz said. "It was about three feet square. How did you get these motorcycles up here?"

The young man, Victor, explained that he and a friend had carried them up five stories, ten flights of stairs. He said the threat of theft by parking them on the street was too great.

"He started the motorcycle up right in his apartment just to prove it ran," Fritz said. "Luckily he was a young guy with no family. He actually spoke a few words of English because he watched American television programs."

They bought the Harley for about eight hundred dollars and arranged to keep the bike stored in the apartment until shipping could be arranged.

From there, it was off to another motorcycle collector, this one a father and son who ran a semilegitimate repair and restoration shop in the basement of their building.

"The son would restore bikes to a pretty low quality, but at least he got them back on the road again," Fritz said. "They had a few Indians, but they had a strange method for negotiating the price. It was early evening, and they said we should go to the café to have a glass of vodka. At three a.m., we left the café, having consumed five bottles of vodka! But we bought a nice Indian 741 for about twelve hundred dollars.

"We were in pretty bad shape the next day though."

They also inspected another Indian, a 1919 model, in another fellow's apartment. Fritz said the bike was very nice for its age, at least what he could see of it.

"The guy hadn't paid his electric bill for his apartment, so the lights had been turned off," Fritz said. "I had to inspect the bike using a cigarette lighter as a flashlight.

"Even though we really wanted the bike, we could never come to an agreement on price, so we left his apartment empty-handed."

They also bought another rare BMW R75 complete with a sidecar. An interesting feature of that sidecar was its wheel was driven with a driveshaft from the rear wheel of the motorcycle, making it two-wheel drive and excellent for the duty that model performed with General Rommel's assault on Africa.

After a busy three days, Fritz and Ben returned to Estonia to talk with the Aktion P owner. Another four days of talks failed to have the Mercedes in their hands, so Fritz packed for a flight to the United States the next morning. Reuter, who had stayed in Moscow to hunt for more cars, would meet Fritz at the airport the next day to fly back with him. But the Aktion P, the prize they had sought, still eluded them. Ben had decided to stay in Estonia to try to secure its purchase one more time. Fritz went to bed early, and Ben went to the owner's home in the countryside for more negotiations.

"At five in the morning, Ben comes bounding into the hotel room shouting, 'We got the car. We got the car. Get up! You have to figure out how to get the car to America,'" Fritz said. "I told him that if he was kidding me, I'd kill him."

Ben negotiated a complicated deal that included "a lot of cash," Fritz's old Mercedes station wagon, and an American boarding school education for the man's daughter.

The real gem in Victor's collection was this 1943 Harley-Davidson WLA 42, which he and a friend had carried up to the fifth floor so it wouldn't be stolen. To show Fritz how well the bike ran, he started it up right in the apartment! *Dick Fritz*

"What?" Fritz asked, still in a slumber. But once Ben explained the deal, and that the man's daughter's education was his highest priority, it made sense.

When Reuter arrived at the airport from Moscow to meet Fritz and he wasn't there, Reuter knew something was up and went to the motel where Fritz and Ben were staying.

The third trip a few weeks later was virtually dedicated to packing up the Aktion P in order to sneak it out of the country under the cover of darkness. The car's exit from Estonia was complicated but included two rented cargo planes, an eighteen-wheeler, several delivery vans, payments to the general manager of an airport, hush money, and a foggy night, making their escape that much more hazardous. But after several stressful days trying to stay out of the sight of undesirable Estonians, the car and its new owners escaped and were headed for the United States. Between the purchase of four motorcycles and the Aktion P, the third trip had been the charm.

The group, now energized from their daring purchase and escape, made a total of seven trips to the former Soviet Union looking for cars, motorcycles, and even World War II aircraft.

"On one trip, Reuter, Peter the Swede, and I flew across Siberia to the Kuril Islands to see if there [were] any World War II American warplanes to be had," Fritz said. "It was somewhat frightening flying to Petropavlovsk on the Kamchatka Peninsula across the eleven time zones of Russia, over the nothingness of Siberia.

"We took a two-hour helicopter ride to Seviro Kurilsk, a city of forty-five hundred on the third northernmost island, and drove to some of the old Japanese airbases that had existed there before the Russian occupation," Fritz said. "They did find a number of dismantled King Cobras, Japanese Zeros, and Betty bombers, as well as old tanks and military trucks, but we decided not to pursue them. There was just some bad feeling we had about the area, and we just didn't feel safe being there."

They returned to Moscow and Saint Petersburg to search for more motorcycles. One gentleman they met invited them over to his large basement to see his collection. On the way there, he drove them on a piece of elevated roadway that was about one thousand feet across and six or seven miles long.

"He explained to us that underneath the road they were driving on was every type of military vehicle you could think of—trucks, tanks, airplanes—and about one million people," Fritz said. "This was the Memorial Highway that contained the remains of the city of Leningrad [Saint Petersburg] after the Germans had attacked. That was a sobering experience.

"When we made it to his country house, he showed us a very nice Harley-Davidson and a nice Mercedes 170, both of which we purchased. But he was a tough negotiator because he never reduced his price but instead kept adding other items into the deal.

"As we were writing up the deal, he mentioned that it was a shame we weren't there six weeks earlier, because he had just sold two Auto Union Grand Prix race cars.

"We said, 'What?' Then he showed us the photo of the two rear-engined cars in the basement and explained that he had just sold them six weeks earlier to a collector from Europe.

"Can you believe that? These are the priceless cars that Audi restored and displays today."

The Mercedes, which was purchased for $19,000, never made it to the States. Fritz figures the car was probably stolen before it reached the dock in what was probably an "inside job" among the shipping agents.

On another trip, the trio was invited into a barn that was loaded with old motorcycles and parts.

This military 1943 BMW R75 came complete with Steib sidecar. It was purchased for $3,350 from a man named Igor about 30 miles from Moscow. *Dick Fritz*

"This guy had a two-story building stacked with parts, and they were fairly neat and organized," Fritz said. "Upstairs, he had gas tanks lined up, wheels, sidecars, fenders, handlebars, and frames. Downstairs, he had complete bikes. It was an impressive collection, but his prices were very high, so we didn't buy anything from him."

A number of the bikes they looked at were sitting outside and too far gone to make good investments. One they did purchase was a BMW R75 with a sidecar that had been sitting in a field with grass growing through its frame and wheels.

In all, Fritz believes he inspected at least a hundred motorcycles and purchased just fourteen. Only three of the fourteen ran, but all of them were nearly 80 to 90 percent complete.

The least amount of money they paid for a motorcycle was two hundred dollars, and the most they paid was four thousand dollars, for a bright-green Indian. They figured that if they could buy a motorcycle and have it transported to the United States for an average of two thousand dollars each, there would be a healthy profit when they were sold for seven thousand dollars or eight thousand dollars each.

Fritz wishes they had purchased more BMW R75s with sidecars. These turned out to be the most valuable and desirable to buyers in the United States.

Probably the nicest motorcycle purchased by the Americans was this 1943 BMW R75 built for the Afrika Korps. If you look carefully between the handlebars and the seat, you can see a large dome, which is the cover for the special desert air cleaner used by the Germans in the North African campaign. They paid $4,000 for the bike. *Dick Fritz*

Another BMW R75 military motorcycle equipped for desert operations. This photo better shows the large air cleaner cover that some thought looked like a spare German army helmet. This bike was found in a field behind a summer house near Saint Petersburg. The BMWs built for sidecar use had a power take-off driving the sidecar's rear wheel, giving this bike two-wheel drive. They paid $3,350 for the bike. *Dick Fritz*

"These were made for the Nazis fighting in the Sahara Desert, and they had a few special features to cope with the environment, such as supplemental air filters. The extra-large air cleaner looked like a Nazi helmet that sat on top of the gas tank," Fritz said. "Air would come up inside the helmet and then down through a tube through the center of the gas tank and into the carburetor.

"These bikes were built for the desert, but when Rommel was defeated, they were shipped to Russia for the German offensive against the Russians on the Eastern Front. When Germany was defeated, all those bikes were just left there.

Fritz bought this 1943 Indian 741 military model from a man named Sasha for $2,200. It was discovered in a basement near Moscow. *Dick Fritz*

"After the war, Russia took everything of value they could out of Germany, including the contents of the BMW factory. Soon, Russia was pumping out BMW clones, which they still continue to build versions of today.

"We sold the BMWs for between eight thousand and ten thousand dollars, when they were probably worth closer to twenty thousand dollars."

And even though they didn't buy any of the spare parts they discovered, Fritz said that they did see piles of spare parts as well. "The most interesting was an Ariel Square Four engine and a sidecar with an opening in the front that looked like a jet plane," he said.

This military Harley-Davidson was purchased for $2,900 from a second-floor apartment. Fritz said it was one of the nicest bikes they purchased and still had much of the special military equipment installed. *Dick Fritz*

"We really didn't make any money on the bikes, but it did pay for our trips."

All fourteen bikes were crated and packed into one twenty-foot storage container that was put on a ship in Tallinn and arrived in New York a few weeks later.

Total shipping cost was about $2,000.

Soon after the bike booty arrived at Fritz's Amerispec shop in Danbury, Connecticut, he brought a couple of his discovered motorcycles to the huge Super Sunday motorcycle rally held nearby. The bikes were a hit.

Instead of marketing the motorcycles in *Hemmings Motor News* or the *New York Times*, all the bikes were sold through word of mouth. Fritz said that they were satisfied with the profits their motorcycle sales generated but admits that today, with the extensive use of the Internet, he would utilize sites such as eBay to generate a higher return.

Fritz has had many years to reflect since taking the most dynamic barn-finding expedition of a lifetime in 1992. First, he believes there are still places around the world that offer treasure hunters opportunities to search and buy long-forgotten vehicles.

"I think Africa probably still has World War II relics," he said, "especially if you were hunting for motorcycles like the BMW R75 and aircraft. Things certainly wouldn't rust very badly there. And I believe that treasures still exist in Russia."

Fritz believes that searching for cars in Russia would be safer now than it was more than sixteen years ago.

Russians are good negotiators, Fritz said. "They are calculating, rational, and very intelligent," he said. "Remember, some of the best chess players in the world are Russians."

The most unusual negotiation Fritz was involved in was for a motorcycle. Negotiations had ended because Fritz thought the asking price was too high.

"Then the seller pulled me aside and informed him that for this price, it included a Russian girl. I said, 'What do you mean a Russian girl?' The seller said, 'We have a lot of Russian girls here. If you want for one night, two nights, she's included in the price.'

"I said, 'No, thank you very much. All we are after is cars and motorcycles; we don't want to bring anything else home.'"

Fritz and his colleagues feel best about the boarding school education they were able to give to the daughter of the Estonian Aktion P owner. She attended two years at an exclusive private school in Massachusetts and, in her early thirties and again living in Estonia, still stays in touch with him.

Now that Fritz is older and hopefully wiser, has he thought about making another Russian treasure hunt, knowing the risks involved?

"It does occur to me occasionally," he said. "But it's usually after a large meal where I've had too much to drink. In the middle of the night, I wake up in a sweat having just dreamed about going back there.

"I've actually heard of a rare Mercedes 500 fastback called the Autobahn Carrier that is sitting in Iran. It was built to celebrate speed record runs on the Autobahn and once belonged to the Shah of Iran. I've seen pictures of it, but am I going there? No way! Maybe someday the conditions will exist to safely go over there and get that car, but I don't see that happening soon.

"With all the dangers we encountered—potential theft, kidnapping, death, mafia, KGB, and disorganized crime—the modern-day treasure hunt was worthwhile only because of the Aktion P, which was quite valuable. I wouldn't relish being killed over a BMW motorcycle.

"Because you're only crazy once."

SAME BIKE, DIFFERENT BASEMENT

BY ZACK MILLER

I think it's possible, when young, to have a motorcycle experience so affecting that it remains with you the rest of your life. A sort of two-wheeled first kiss. The world shifts, tilts, and a general longing transforms to a specific desire.

I think this happened to me when I was twelve. We had a visitor in our garage that summer, a 1970 Ducati Mark 3 D. It belonged to Bruce, a friend of my father's and something of a rock star, at least in my eyes and by the standards of east-central Iowa. Tall, thin, with long hair and stylish seventies clothes, he variously arrived at our house in a Pantera, a Continental Mk III, or a 4-4-2 reputedly "set up for drag racing." Bruce owned stereo shops and music stores. He went target shooting with not one but a pair of nickel-plated .357s. It was hard to believe my father actually knew someone this cool.

I don't recall when the Ducati arrived or why, but I do remember seeing it for the first time, centered in the only open space in our otherwise crammed two-stall garage. Dad explained that Bruce bought it and immediately had it modified before ever riding it. I could see a velocity stack, a matte-black

Though sold and titled as a 1970 model, this Mark 3 D was likely built in 1969. Some Mark 3s exported to the United States had the Scrambler tank and tall bars rather than the "coffin" tank and clip-ons worn by their sportier European-spec brothers. *Zack Miller*

megaphone exhaust, and a special gold paint job. I could only imagine the trick bits that must have been hidden away inside the engine. Apparently, the diminutive Duc was so mind-bendingly fast that it scared the bejesus out of Bruce the first time he gave it a hard twist. Now the demon was cooling its heels in our garage. What luck!

My dad rode it only a few times over its short stay with us, preferring the relative refinement and quiet of his old AJS twin. Madness, to my thinking. But then he also thought the Pantera "rode like a lumber wagon." For my part, I logged hours in the saddle, sitting in our garage and imagining myself blowing down the road at supra-legal speeds, a Phil Spector wall-of-megaphone sound in my wake.

The Desmo, as Dad called it, went away as unexpectedly as it had arrived, recalled by Bruce and gone forever for all I knew. Time sped on and so did I, first aboard a Honda CL160 and a short-lived Kawasaki triple while still in high school, then astride a further succession of Kawasakis while in college in the early eighties. But like a first crush, that little Ducati never quite left my mind. For years, I had a recurring conversation with my father:

33

Me: So, do you think Bruce still has that Ducati?

Him: That Desmo?

Me: Yeah, the Desmo.

Him: Maybe. Why?

Me: Think he'd sell it if he had it?

Him: Maybe.

Me: Why don't you ask him next time you talk to him?

Him: I haven't talked to Bruce in years.

Me: A good excuse to touch base. "How's the wife? Do you still have a wife? A Pantera? Do you want to sell that Ducati?"

Him: Yeah, I should call him.

Repeat every few months for a few years.

Then one day, unbidden and out of the blue, the old man calls. "I talked to Bruce the other day."

"Bruce who?"

"Which Bruce do you think?"

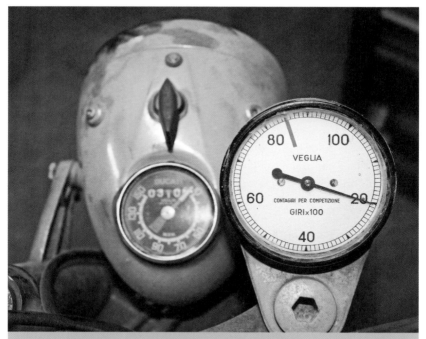

This Veglia tach is a very desirable period accessory. Note the 8,500-rpm redline. Stratospheric for the day, courtesy of Ducati's desmodromic valve actuation. *Zack Miller*

Twelve-year-old Nate does his best steely eyed impression of what the old man must have looked like all those years ago. *Zack Miller*

"Cool Bruce?"

"Yeah. Bruce with the Ducati."

"Does he still have it?"

"Yep. Been parked in his basement for fifteen years."

Fifteen. Years. Unbelievable. How could anyone own something so cool, so exotic, and not have ridden it for fifteen years? It was like being married to an Italian supermodel but sleeping in a separate bedroom every night. I couldn't comprehend it. I knew this machine deserved better.

"Does he want to sell it?"

"He said you should call him."

Give me that number.

I called, skipped the how's-the-wife-and-Pantera niceties, and quickly got to the point.

"Dad says you'd be willing to sell the Ducati."

"Sure."

"How much do you think you want for it?"

"Well, I'll sell it to you for the same price I offered it to your dad."

"Okay. So how much was that?"

I couldn't believe the number. It must have been the price offered my dad in 1975 or something when the Desmo was a five-year-old, weirdo Italian thing that eleven people in all of Iowa had heard of. In the summer of 1988, the asking price was a killer deal. I confirmed that I'd drive to Iowa from Minnesota to retrieve it that weekend.

Bruce lived in a tidy ranch-style house, and, just as Dad had reported, the Ducati was tucked away in a corner of the basement. The bike was thick with dust but showed a scant 3,105 miles on the odometer. It still wore the megaphone exhaust and velocity stack I remembered, and it had a lovely little Veglia accessory tach mounted atop the triple tree. We horsed it up the steps and rolled it into the back of my truck.

Beaming, I hit the road back to Minnesota. I felt like I had a pickup bed full of Krugerrands. People passed me on the highway staring at the Duc with what I imagined to be considerable envy ("My God, Madge, that young buck has a 350 Desmo in the back of that truck!") but was probably closer to pity ("Poor bastard. Do you think that's a motorcycle under that grime?").

Once home, the Desmo was rolled into its new basement lair, where a bit of probing and prodding revealed it to be basically sound and largely unmolested, save for some fool having bobbed the rear fender a couple inches—seemingly with a bow saw—for God knows what reason.

There the Duc sat while I finished a slow, ground-up rebuild of a Ducati Pantah. In the meantime, I went back to school, got married, bought a house, rolled the Desmo into that basement, changed jobs, had a kid, finished the Pantah, had another kid. Imagine the hands of a clock spinning wildly around the dial like in some silent-movie representation of passing years and you'll begin to get a sense where this story is going.

Fast forward a bit further still, and I find myself talking to Tom Cotter about this book.

"You know, Tom, I have a story I think I'd like to write for your book."

Kindly, he agrees to let me.

So I'm driving home from work one day thinking about this story, the story of a very special Ducati left to molder in some dude's basement for fifteen years. Still shaking my head in disbelief, my mind wanders back to the summer of 1988 when I rescued it. 1988. Thirty years ago. My reverie is stopped dead in its tracks. Thirty. Years. Unbelievable. How could anyone own something so cool, so exotic, and not have ridden it . . .

No. Don't even ask. Not for sale.

A BEAST OF HARLEY

As hard as it might be to believe, once upon a time, motorcycles were faster than dragsters in the quarter-mile. It was in the early 1950s, and Wally Parks's new National Hot Rod Association (NHRA) was still in its infancy.

During those early days, bikes offered a power-to-weight ratio superior to even the hottest drag cars of the day.

One person who was particularly interested in keeping bikes in the fastest time-of-the-day category was a young speed demon named Chet Herbert.

Herbert was born in Arizona but grew up in Southern California. His parents had hoped he would pursue a career in the music industry and bought the youngster a trumpet. Herbert quickly tired of the trumpet and traded it for a motor scooter. His life has been in the fast lane ever since.

Herbert traded up from the scooter and eventually rode a Harley on which he terrorized the streets of Los Angeles in the mid-1940s.

"I heard about a guy who worked at a Harley dealership who was selling the fastest bike on the street," said Herbert, who at eighty was still operating speed shops in Santa Ana and Chino, California. "So I bought it, but I started to change it more for racing."

Herbert was a tough competitor, but soon after purchasing the Harley, his toughness would be tested. In 1948, he contracted polio, which left him paralyzed from the chest down. He was just twenty years old. From a racing standpoint, it took him out of the saddle, but from a development standpoint, he never wavered. Herbert began to develop and engineer parts for bikes and cars from his wheelchair.

California hot rod pioneer Chet Herbert was the fastest man in the world in quarter-mile drag races in the early 1950s with this bike, known as *The Beast*. *Tom Cotter*

"It kind of motivated him to become an innovator," said Herbert's son Doug, who followed his father's love for speed and became an NHRA Top Fuel driver. "He's never been afraid of anything; he just goes after it.

"He was in the hospital for a long time and started to read about how the Germans were using nitromethane to power torpedoes. He knew when he got out of the hospital, he had to get his hands on some of that stuff."

From his wheelchair, Herbert continued to modify the motorcycle he could no longer ride. It was coined *The Beast* by track announcers because of its ungainly appearance. The 1947 Knucklehead used a VL frame and front forks because they were lighter and more aerodynamic than other frames. But it required fish-plating, which was steel plates welded at crucial points so it wouldn't twist with all the torque off the line.

"I used a pre-1933 Harley-Davidson frame because it was a single stringer frame," Chet Herbert said. "It was better for racing than the double-stringer frames that later Harleys used."

Herbert's *Beast* rode through the traps at 103 miles per hour once at the Santa Ana Drags with a rider he no longer remembers. Some more modifications and another rider, Al Keys, and *The Beast* was clocked at 121.62 miles per hour, the fastest any vehicle had ever accelerated through the quarter-mile to that point.

No other car or bike could touch Herbert's Harley in the early 1950s. Here an article in a 1950 issue of *Cycle* tells of the bike's nearly 130-mile-per-hour run at the Santa Ana, California, drag strip. *Chet Hebert collection*

It was July 1950, and Herbert was ready to set another record but knew it would take more than pump fuel to accomplish this task. His crew members mixed up a concoction of alcohol, water, castor oil, and the German torpedo trick—nitromethane—and filled the bike's homemade gas tank using rubber gloves to avoid being burned by the potent mixture in the event of a spill. The fuel was fed to a huge pair of carburetors that had come off an Offenhauser midget race engine.

The Beast had already been ridden to 128 miles per hour at the El Mirage dry lake, but Herbert was seeking domination on the paved quarter-mile. When rider Ted Irio mounted *The Beast*, he held on tight. The bike had no clutch or starter, so it was kick-started on a stand, which was no easy task since it had a 13:1 compression ratio.

Eyewitnesses that day remember that even though Irio started off in second gear, the bike's rear tire wouldn't stop spinning and ultimately caught fire as it left the line. Irio had to back off on the throttle until the tire stopped spinning, then slowly accelerate as it gained traction. *The Beast* fishtailed all the way down the drag strip, and spectators from the stands were treated to a record-shattering run of 129 miles per hour. But the fans were also confused because all they saw was a cloud of dust at the far end of the strip.

Irio was going fast, so fast that he couldn't stop *The Beast*. He went on a wild cool-down ride, catapulting end-over-end until he finally came to rest, thankfully unhurt, in a pile of dirt far beyond the finish line.

The Beast was rebuilt and continued to race at drag strips and dry lake events until Herbert decided to sell it.

"I raced it for a couple of years but decided to put it up for sale in 1952," Herbert said. "I put an ad in one of the cycle magazines for fifteen hundred dollars. At the time, I was really getting away from bikes and getting more into cars.

"This rich kid from Chicago called me and wanted to buy it. He and another rich kid with a hopped-up roadster had a bet with each other. The kid with the roadster said, 'You get any kind of motorcycle, and I'll blow your doors off in the quarter-mile.' So the other kid bought my bike and the bet was called off. That roadster would have been lucky to go one hundred five miles per hour, and *The Beast* would go twenty-five miles per hour faster."

The senior Herbert continued to develop speed parts. He bought a lathe from Sears and began grinding his own camshafts for cars and motorcycles.

He invented the roller cam and lifter setup, which have been used by racers ever since.

"Once people realized how much horsepower those roller cams produced, there were fifty people lined up at his door to have custom camshafts ground," Doug said. Herbert also started the Zoomie Header business.

Herbert opened a speed shop that operates to this day but never stopped building fast cars. He built numerous dragsters and Bonneville streamliners that continued to set speed records for decades.

Through a lifetime of success, though, he never forgot his first bike, *The Beast*. Son Doug tracked it down and bought it back.

"It was in terrible shape and all disassembled," Doug said. "It sat around his shop for a long time before I asked him if I could restore it.

"I took it last summer [2008]."

Today *The Beast* is in Doug Herbert's race shop in Lincolnton, North Carolina, going through a slow and thorough restoration.

"I want to restore it in my dad's honor and display it in my showroom," he said. "And I'd like to bring it to the drags and let people see a bike that was once the fastest thing on wheels. It's not very often that they get to see such an early bike."

THE WORLD'S FASTEST INDIAN

How does it feel to be the keeper of the most famous motorcycle in the world?

Ask Tom Hensley. His family has owned Burt Munro's Indian streamliner since way before it became famous. Hensley manages the bike as part of a small motorcycle collection for the family, in honor not only of Munro, but also of Hensley's late brother, Dean.

First about Munro. If you haven't seen the 2005 movie *The World's Fastest Indian*, starring Anthony Hopkins, set aside your next available evening and rent the movie. To anyone interested enough to leaf through a book titled *Tom Cotter's Best Barn-Find Collector Car Tales*, the movie is a must-see.

Munro was born in Invercargill, New Zealand, in 1899 and from childhood was interested in all things mechanical: cars, trucks, airplanes, boats, and motorcycles. Living on his family's farm did not give him much opportunity to see many vehicles. Growing up in a remote area, though, did teach him that he needed to be self-sufficient; he sometimes had to build parts from scratch if he wanted to get a job done.

In 1920, as a twenty-one-year-old, Munro purchased a brand-new Indian Scout motorcycle, which had a 600cc engine and a top speed of fifty-five miles per hour. This modest speed only kept the young man intrigued for so long, and by 1926, he had already begun modifying the bike.

His prowess in modifying and riding bikes won some acclaim. At one point, he competed in professional speedway races and eventually set seven New Zealand speed records, beginning in 1938.

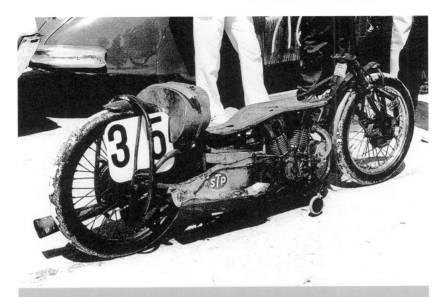

It's hard to believe that at one time, this was a stock Indian Scout. Munro burned up speedways in his native New Zealand in the late 1930s and 1940s before setting his sights on land-speed records. *Photo from Petersen Publishing Company. Courtesy of Hensley Family Collection*

Munro set his sights on a land land-speed-record and traveled to the Bonneville Salt Flats in Utah for the annual Speed Weeks trials to investigate the scene and plan his strategy.

He continued to modify his bike, and in 1962, with its engine punched out from 600cc to 800cc, Munro set a record of 178.95 miles per hour. In 1966, he set another record.

The people who frequent Bonneville's Speed Weeks took a liking to Munro. They knew he was broke, but they also knew he was a genius. Folks befriended him, loaned him tools, and gave him spare parts and a place to sleep.

The Pierce family was one who took Munro in. They were from San Gabriel, California, and owned Pierce Indian, one of the leading parts and service centers after the Indian factory closed its doors in 1953. During the ten years that Munro competed at Bonneville, the Pierces allowed him to store his bike at their facility when he traveled back home to New Zealand. They also gave him parts and allowed him to use their shop to work on his bike prior to bringing it to Bonneville.

"The Pierces sponsored Burt in 1967, which is why the fiberglass bodywork had 'Pierce Indian of San Gabriel' painted on the bike's tail," Hensley said.

"Burt started to run on nitro when he came to the States, so every winter when he brought his engine back home to rebuild, the Pierces bottled up nitromethane in wine bottles and sent them along, because he couldn't get it in New Zealand." The nitro is also why he kept burning holes in pistons, because he was casting them himself in the backyard from probably inferior materials.

In addition to pistons, Munro made his own cylinder barrels, flywheels, and numerous other items. In fact, the hoops that supported the fiberglass body were actually recycled fence post stakes. Munro also built connecting rods out of old Ford tractor axles.

Munro's effort in 1967 seems to have brought all the lessons of the previous years together. If racing was a young man's sport, Munro knew nothing about it; he was sixty-eight years old and his motorcycle was forty-seven.

By now his Indian's engine had grown to 950cc. When his turn to race finally came, he turned in a two-way average of 183.586 miles per hour, finally breaking the under-1,000cc world record.

After having been raced for a half-century, Burt Munro's famous Indian was at first displayed at a dealership in the 1970s but eventually put out to pasture next to a storage building. This is the condition of the 1920 Scout when acquired by the late Dean Hensley in 1984. *Photo from Petersen Publishing Company. Courtesy of Hensley Family Collection*

Munro ran at Bonneville a couple more times, but he finally hung up his helmet in 1970, when he was seventy-one years old. When he left the United States for the last time, he gave his beloved Indian to the Pierce family as a thank-you for all the years of assistance.

For a while, the Pierces displayed the World's Fastest Indian in their showroom, then relegated it to the warehouse, and ultimately to the elements outside, where the decades of Munro's loving modifications slowly deteriorated into the ground.

Enthusiast Gordy Clark purchased the Indian from the Pierces but just put it into storage. Remember, at this time, Munro's motorcycle was just a beat-up old racer, not very interesting to even the most serious motorcycle collectors. This was before the modern antique bike craze really took off. It was a curiosity, nothing more.

Enter Dean Hensley. Dean, Tom Hensley's older brother, was a rising motorcycle racing star. At just eighteen years old, he was already making a name for himself on the road-racing circuit. One day, he was racing at the El Sonora track when he wrecked and was run over by another bike.

"When my parents got the call about my brother, I rode to the hospital with them," said Tom Hensley, who was twelve years old at the time. "Hell, I didn't even know what the word 'paralyzed' meant. They had him in traction but managed to somehow drop him to the floor when he first arrived. But even though he was paralyzed from the chest down, he bounced back like a flower."

Dean Hensley and Tom, who at thirteen became his brother's full-time caregiver, went into business.

"He went to the fine art school at Pasadena City College to learn how to pinstripe and paint flames," Tom said. "One thing led to another, and we began selling antique-looking mirrors that we sold to pubs." According to Tom, the mirror business was earning $2 million a year in the early 1980s.

"He had known about the Indian for years," Tom said, referring to the historic bike that had been stored in a neglected state among Gordy Clark's three-hundred-bike collection. Dean purchased the bike in 1986, soon after selling the antique mirror company.

"He had gone to an auction, maybe it was at Hershey, and saw that old streamliners were beginning to sell for substantial money," Tom said. "That's when he decided to try to buy the old Burt Munro bike."

After the purchase, Munro's Indian sat around for a few years as Dean gathered enough information and parts to begin restoration. "The body was beaten down like nobody's business," said Tom. "As we say out here on the West Coast: it was crusty. We have detailed photos of the restoration. Since the bike sat outside for years, four frame tubes filled with water and rusted out."

Tom said that the photographs are proof they own the actual Indian. He said there are collectors in New Zealand who claim to own the actual World's Fastest Indian, but he said that was actually a chassis mockup that Munro used to test his engines. Tom Hensley said Munro's bike never left the United States once it was shipped here in 1962. Dean Hensley had the bike restored by master restorer Steve Huntsinger.

The bike was never completely reassembled because Dean wanted to be able to sit on the bike at startup. So special hand controls were adapted and half the body was not installed.

"The left side of the body hung on my garage wall for twenty years," said Tom. "The fiberglass had settled, so getting it fitting back together was like fixing Marty Feldman's eyes. We had to mount it to a board, let it sit in the sun, and every day turn the set screws one-quarter turn to get the body to move back into place."

Dean brought his now-restored Indian streamliner to a Davenport, Iowa, swap meet and decided to start the bike after it hadn't run in twenty years. They had built an Indy-type starter that mounted on the countershaft, and Dean could operate it with hand controls.

"They had never detuned the engine, so they were still running high compression," Tom said. "My brother revved it up running on methanol and snapped a connecting rod." Afterward, the bike was relegated to a static show bike.

Sadly, Dean Hensley, who had worked so hard and accomplished so much in the worlds of art, business, and motorcycles, was killed in an auto accident in May 1992. Tom continued to show the bike after his brother's passing, but other collectors made him upset.

"What pissed me off was that I had collectors trying to buy my brother's bikes even before I could get him buried," he said. "So, I said, 'You know what guys? You guys ain't getting shit.' That's why I've kept all his stuff." A big brother is a big brother—Tom keeps the bike out of love and respect for Dean.

Besides Munro's Indian, the Hensley family collection includes the original Globe of Death theatrical Indian; an original Isle of Man overhead-cam prototype racer; Gene Ryan's factory overhead valve hillclimber; and the last Indian to win at Ascot Park.

Another memento from Dean is the 1958 Ford Ranchero equipped with hand controls. "I drove it just the other day," Tom said.

In the spring of 2011, Tom received a phone call from the organizers of the Pebble Beach Concours d'Elegance. They said if he could prepare the streamliner to running condition, he could enter it in the prestigious show.

"We were already in the process of getting the bike running with new rods and pistons when Pebble Beach called," he said. "They said it had to be in running condition in order to come to the show, so we built brand-new cylinders from scratch and had the bodywork fitted exactly the way Munro had it mounted when he ran for the record in 1967."

By August, the bike was completed. The Pebble Beach organizers conducted a thorough analysis of the bike's restoration, making sure it was authentic before being invited to be displayed on the lawn. It was displayed at Pebble Beach with only half the bodywork mounted. "Once you mount the entire body, all the work and craftsmanship of the frame and engine is hidden."

Slight modifications were made so the bike could be started in the event it was invited to the trophy presentation. For instance, Munro had no carburetor venturi, making idling impossible. "It was like sucking soda through a funnel," Tom said. "It wouldn't run at low rpms."

It's a good thing Tom got the bike to operate, because it was called onto the stage for a first-place trophy in the racing motorcycle category. "We started it up," he said. "My brother was the last person to run it, and almost twenty-five years later, I was the next."

Having won the show of all shows, the Hensley family is considering what to do next. "This is not my bike, it belongs to my family's collection," Tom is quick to point out. "I have two sisters and a brother. They have been gracious enough to help keep the collection of my brother's bikes together."

They are now considering selling the collection, which includes about a dozen bikes, as a single unit. Because New Zealanders consider Burt Munro to be their John Wayne, I'd be surprised if someone down there didn't buy it. But parting with the family collection won't be easy. Tom truly cares who owns these bikes next.

"After all, this is my brother's legacy," he said.

FROM THE ISLE OF MAN TO A MIDWESTERN BARN

BY SOMER HOOKER

In the sixties, one of the hottest contested classes in Europe and Japan was the 50cc class. 50cc bikes and scooters were the bread and butter of the manufacturers. Some extreme technology was utilized, such as nine-speed gearboxes, to help keep them in their power band. At the zenith of the class, some manufacturers went to fifteen speeds.

I have always had an affinity for small displacement motorcycles. Once, while at a motorcycle swap meet, I was looking at a Honda 90 that had been run at the Salt Flats. In the course of the conversation, the owner mentioned that he knew of a small Suzuki racer. I expressed interest and gave him my contact information, fully expecting to later see a Suzuki X-6 with a café fairing. When the photos arrived, I could not believe my eyes! It was a genuine Suzuki 50cc GP bike with a number 1 plate on it.

Trying to hide my excitement, I called and expressed my interest. There was a catch. This was part of a Suzuki dealership that had gone under. Everything had been moved into a barn, and the owners had moved west to open a curio shop. My guy would have to track them down. He later reported back that he had to buy everything, including parts, but he was going forward. He named a price on the 50cc Suzuki, which was accepted.

At the same time, I started doing some research and learned that this was probably Hugh Anderson's GP bike that had won the Isle of Man. It was

Most bikes of this vintage were cut up and discarded after being retired from track service, but this one managed to survive. *Mike Cady*

common in Japanese motorcycle manufacturing to forego any sentiment about the past and concentrate on future development. At the end of the year, many GP bikes were cut up. Somehow this one had survived, maybe because it was number 1?

The owner later called me and announced, "I found out that this is worth more." I swallowed hard and said, "What price are you thinking?" The amount he stated this time had doubled. Numerous thoughts run through your mind when confronted with this type of situation. Do you curse him and tell him, "We had a deal!" Do you counter with an offer for less? Or do you do what I did and just say okay? I knew it was worth more and rare, and I also knew that if you counter, you may no longer have a deal. I sensed that countering could cost me the bike.

I made payment for it and arranged to have a friend pick it up when he was going through the area. I took delivery and was extremely pleased, although I did notice that it had no compression. It was not uncommon for GP bikes to be gutted before letting them go. The inner workings were considered top secret.

The bike was so small I displayed it on my desk. Visitors were always curious, and I would jokingly tell them that this was the bike I rode before I had my growth spurt (I'm six-foot-four). I sent pictures to Hugh Anderson, and he said

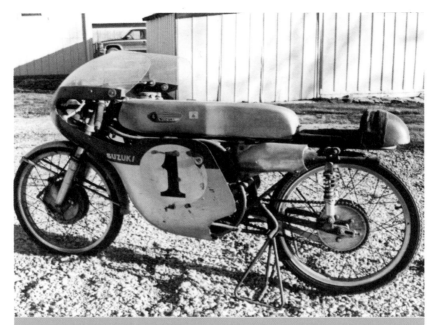

Into the daylight once again, the bike's miniscule dimensions are apparent. Large riders need not apply. Bikes of this size are often used as office or living room "eye candy." *Mike Cady*

it could have been his bike. He allowed that because of his height (maybe five-foot-two) he would squat down during team photos. He was afraid he would be fired for being too tall! I later found a film of what I believed to be this bike being raced at Daytona at some FIM races.

I had a good client and friend from Japan who would come over periodically. He took some photos and later came back and asked if I wanted to sell the bike, and I agreed. He said he would come back and examine it on behalf of his client. After the exam, we surmised that the engine was probably empty, no piston or transmission, and possibly no crank. They later called back and made a counter offer, which I accepted.

It was then revealed to me that the buyer had been one of the riders on the Suzuki team in the sixties and had a complete crank assembly for the bike. Suzuki was excited to learn that he had acquired the bike and said it still had the blueprints for the nine-speed transmission and would make him another one. After traveling around the Isle of Man and then the world to the United States, it would travel back to Japan and be made whole so it could travel around tracks again. Sometimes barn finds go full circle.

The business end. From this vantage point, the rider of this Suzuki navigated the famous Isle of Man race to win first in the 50cc class. *Mike Cady*

Post script: Years later, at a meet, I was approached by a guy who said, "Did you buy a bike from Mike?" I told him yes, and he said, "You know, I saw that bike and offered him double the price."

Sometimes your gut instinct is correct.

MUSCLE CARS
AND
AMERICAN IRON

A TWELVE-YEAR-OLD'S DREAM

It was 1950, and a twelve-year-old boy we'll call Bob was doing what twelve-year-olds did before the age of video games and the Internet: he was being adventurous. He was exploring the rural areas around his home on the outskirts of Columbus, Ohio, and because he was a car-crazy kid, he was searching for old cars.

Walking down the road, he came across an old barn that was just too tempting to pass by; he had to look inside. He snuck across the field, being careful not to let anyone in the nearby farmhouse see him, and he crept up to the building. He peered into the dark barn, and it took a few moments for his eyes to focus, but what he saw was to become the love of his life—a 1932 Ford roadster pickup. He noted that a name was written on the door: Borden's Golden Crest Grade A Milk. Perhaps the truck had been used for milk deliveries or perhaps for hauling materials around the Borden farm.

Ford didn't build many Model B open-cab roadster pickups in 1932, probably for good reason. Most folks wanted a work truck to haul goods or farm supplies, or they wanted a roadster to take on Sunday drives in the summer with the top down. Very few people wanted a convertible truck. Worldwide production of open-cab trucks in 1932 was only about six hundred, making the '32 Ford one of the rarest and most sought-after vintage Fords on the planet. Records show that none of the pickups were manufactured with the famous flathead V-8 engine that had been introduced that year. Instead, all were produced with a four-cylinder Model B engine, a variation of the venerable Model A that had gone out of production the previous year. The trucks could be retrofitted with the V-8 at the dealership if the customer wished to pay an additional fee, which accounts for the few V-8 roadster pickups in existence.

Bob did what any excited kid would do at that moment. He knocked on the door of the farmhouse and asked if the old Ford in the barn was for sale. "Nope," said the farmer. "I'm going to fix it up one day." So Bob said thank you and went about his twelve-year-old adventures on that day in 1950.

But he never forgot about that pickup.

Year after year, decade after decade, Bob thought about that '32 Ford and occasionally inquired with the farmer whether it was for sale yet. Every time the answer was no. Meanwhile, the truck sat obediently in the barn, out of the elements, and out of view from car collectors. It appears that only Bob knew of the pickup's presence.

Now owned by renowned '32 restorer Russell Smith, the roadster pickup will soon undergo an authentic restoration, possibly even with the Borden's Golden Crest Milk livery logo repainted on the doors. *Paul Dobbins*

In 1993, forty years after Bob first discovered the roadster pickup, the old farmer passed away. By now, Bob was a fifty-five-year-old man, but his love for old cars was still as strong as that twelve-year-old kid's. He had heard about the farmer's death, and he discovered that the farmer's son had inherited the '32 Ford. He was finally able to negotiate the purchase after more than half a century of trying. Over the years, Bob had become a car collector, and annually he made the pilgrimage to Hershey, Pennsylvania, for the large parts swap meet there. During one of those trips several years after purchasing the Ford, he was selling parts at one of the booths—1932 Ford parts, in fact—when a gentleman named Russell Smith of Saint Petersburg, Florida, came over to look at Bob's parts on the table. Smith mentioned to Bob that he needed parts to finish the restoration of a 1932 Ford Phaeton, but what he really wanted was a '32 Ford roadster pickup.

Bob mentioned that he had one and showed him a few photos. Smith—who is a renowned 1932 Ford restorer, and whose nickname is Deuce Smith—had to own the car and wouldn't leave Bob's booth until he negotiated its purchase.

Smith restores only the most authentic 1932 Fords, from sedans to his latest, a Wayne-bodied school bus, and he only starts with the very best candidates. He is known for not overly restoring cars but instead making them exactly the way they were produced by Ford Motor Company.

By the time the Hershey swap meet was over, Smith owned the roadster pickup.

It is now in Florida, where Smith is researching the car's history and collecting materials for its restoration.

"When Deuce does a restoration, it is correct," said his friend Paul Dobbins, also of Saint Petersburg, who helped with this story. "If it would be prettier to chrome plate the brass windshield stanchions rather than paint them black like the originals, he'll still paint them black."

Smith has even considered restoring the car in its Borden's dairy livery.

The question is, why, after forty-three years of lusting after an old car, did Bob ultimately sell the car? "He wasn't a twelve-year-old anymore," Dobbins said. "He had owned lots of old cars over the years, and at sixty-five, [he] was beginning to wind down."

Or perhaps the search and discovery of the car was more gratifying than owning it.

FLEA MARKET PHOTOS LEAD TO UNUSUAL, ONE-OFF TRUCK FIND

Jim Degnan already had a unique car transporter, a converted Olds Tornado airport limo, when he saw another one and decided he had to have it. Degnan didn't see the actual hauler, but a picture of it, while flipping through a box of discarded magazine photos at a flea market. It was a Cheetah transporter, custom made by Norm Holtkamp in the early 1960s, and modeled after a high-speed Mercedes-Benz hauler.

There was no guarantee that the car still existed, yet Degnan set out to find it. He guessed that if it was still around, it would be in Southern California, so he started to make some calls.

He first asked his sports car and hot rod buddies to see if they knew the whereabouts of this vehicle. "Then I spoke to Tom Medley, who was the cartoonist for *Hot Rod Magazine*'s Stroker McGurk. Medley knew that Norm Holtkamp was the original builder and that he still lived in California. So I found his phone number and called him," Degnan said.

That's when Degnan got the whole story.

Norm Holtkamp, a former midget racer from northern California, began thinking about building a high-speed race hauler after seeing a Mercedes hauler profiled in a 1950s edition of *Road & Track* magazine. He was intrigued with the concept—especially because the Mercedes hauler, powered by a 300SL engine, could carry the team's W196 Grand Prix car or 300SLR racer from Stuttgart to Le Mans at 105 miles per hour.

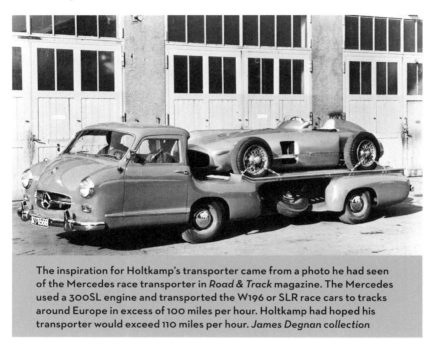

The inspiration for Holtkamp's transporter came from a photo he had seen of the Mercedes race transporter in *Road & Track* magazine. The Mercedes used a 300SL engine and transported the W196 or SLR race cars to tracks around Europe in excess of 100 miles per hour. Holtkamp had hoped his transporter would exceed 110 miles per hour. *James Degnan collection*

As a former driver, crew chief, and tuner, he saw the Mercedes hauler as something of a challenge. He wanted to build a faster one, one that could haul at up to 112 miles per hour.

Holtkamp started his project with a Mercedes 300 sedan chassis because he believed the electric load-leveling suspension would adjust and keep the ride height stable. He added Porsche torsion bars that were manually adjustable but kept the stock Mercedes front and rear axles, spindles, and differential in place.

He purchased the 1960 Chevy El Camino cab new directly from the GM Truck Assembly Plant in Van Nuys, California. The engine he chose came from a 1957 Corvette, hopped up to 300 horsepower, and he mated it with a Chevy three-speed transmission.

The original bodywork (which has changed over the past forty years) was crafted by famed panel beaters Troutman and Barnes of Los Angeles. They made all the body panels, including the full belly pan, from aluminum and designed them to be removable (in as quickly as seven minutes).

Holtkamp finished his creation, the Cheetah, in nine months. He had hoped to begin production of a small number of the haulers, perhaps four or five each year, for weekend racing enthusiasts. But his proposed $16,000 price tag (in 1961!) didn't have racers beating a path to his door.

Holtkamp drove the Cheetah to several West Coast sports car races, hauling the Willment Formula Junior for the Retzloff Racing Team. But he wasn't pleased with the transporter's handling. By one account, Holtkamp once hit the brakes coming down a hill and did a backwards wheelie—the rear wheels came off the ground so far the hauler's nose hit the pavement. It's probably that incident that made him decide to lengthen the wheelbase by a few feet and move the engine rearward toward the center of the vehicle. Sadly, with that change, most of the beautiful Troutman and Barnes bodywork was discarded.

Holtkamp never fully completed the lengthened Cheetah and sold it as a project to California hot rod parts manufacturer Dean Moon sometime in the early 1970s. Moon had the connections and the wherewithal to complete Holtkamp's dream if anyone did. His first planned modification was to replace the Mercedes four-wheel drum brakes with Airheart disc components. That was an ill-fated idea—while the Cheetah was at the Hurst Airheart Company, the 1971 earthquake hit.

Eventually Holtkamp sold his transporter to speed equipment manufacturer Dean Moon. Moon sent the truck to the Hurst Airheart Company for installation of disc brakes. While it was there, the storage building it was in collapsed due to the 1971 Los Angeles earthquake. The transporter, however, did not sustain much damage. *James Degnan collection*

Yet maybe fate wasn't so ill-willed. When the earthquake hit, the building literally fell to pieces around the Cheetah, and except for one small dent, the transporter was virtually untouched. The brake conversion was never completed, however, and the Cheetah was eventually moved back to Moon's shop in Santa Fe Springs. There it sat, outside, on jack stands, for about eighteen years.

Degnan's call to Moon Equipment verified that the vehicle was still there. He also learned that Moon had just passed away, and all the stuff in his buildings was being sold off. In no time, Degnan wrote a check to the estate, and Holtkamp's creation was his. "I had my Olds transporter, so we used a forklift and hoisted the Cheetah onto the back of it," he said. "It must have been quite a sight—so unstable that I would only go thirty-five miles per hour on the freeway all the way home. But I was younger then . . ."

After he got it home, Degnan brought it to a mechanic friend who installed power steering, power brakes, rewired it, and dropped in a standard 350-cubic-inch Chevy engine.

The Cheetah now runs and drives, but Degnan isn't quite ready to break any speed records with it. "I'd be hard-pressed to drive it faster than sixty miles per hour," he said. "It was Holtkamp's desire to build a Mercedes beater—one that could haul race cars to the track in record time, but clearly, this car is not it."

The Cheetah has sat for many years in the back of Degnan's shop. The vehicle still needs all the bodywork completed that was discarded when Holtkamp lengthened the chassis. For Degnan, it's a clear case of "better watch what you wish for, because it might come true." He has the transporter of his dreams, but now what?

1967 SHELBY MUSTANG GT500

A cheeseburger and a plate of pancakes actually helped my friend Jim Maxwell and me purchase a 1967 Shelby Mustang GT500 from the person we thought was the original owner.

Bob Ramsuer was an occasional road racer back in the 1960s and 1970s. A colorful character, he raced an Austin-Healey 3000 before stepping up to a 1966 Shelby GT350. A bad wreck in that car brought his driving career to a halt. But all during this time, Bob operated a little luncheonette in the North Carolina town of Lincolnton.

Bob's restaurant, which closed for good around Thanksgiving 2006 because he was getting tired, was famous with locals who would come, eat, and listen to Bob give his opinion on nearly any subject.

Most of those locals didn't know that Bob still owned a unique car, even though the walls of the diner were festooned with photos of Bob's road racing exploits. After all, he drove a Dodge minivan; surely, his car days were over.

Not quite.

I met Bob when I worked at Charlotte Motor Speedway. I was one of a handful of people who knew that behind a small vacant house that Bob owned a few blocks away, sitting without a cover, was a GT500. I had never actually seen the car, but on occasion, Bob mentioned to me that he owned the special Mustang and that people were always bugging him to buy it.

I had first heard about the car in the mid-1980s, when GT500s weren't the hot collector cars they are today. Then, about ten years later, I purchased an

When Bob Ramsuer finally decided to sell his wife's Shelby GT500, I'm glad he chose me and my friend Jim Maxwell as its new owners. The car sat in this backyard for decades and was well known by collectors, but nobody ever made Bob a fair offer. *Tom Cotter*

old NASCAR stock car from Bob's son, Stuart, who was broke and hanging up his helmet on a once-hopeful NASCAR career.

"How's that Shelby doing, Bob?" I asked as I purchased the rough old stock car.

"It's just sitting there in the yard," he said.

"Want to sell it?" I asked.

"Nope!"

So I stored that car away in my memory bank for another decade.

Finally, after selling the 289 Cobra chronicled in *The Cobra in the Barn* at the 2005 RM Auction in Monterey, my friend Jim and I were hot to find another Shelby barn find.

"You know," I said to Jim, "I'll bet old Bob Ramsuer still has that GT500 he's told me about for so long. I haven't ever seen it, but he's a good guy, and I don't think he's pulling my leg." So I drove forty-five minutes to Lincolnton for breakfast one morning.

"Tom, what the heck are you doing here?" yelled Bob from behind the lunch counter. "How many years has it been?"

Knowing that Bob was a Ford racing fan, I presented him with a copy of the Holman-Moody book that I wrote several years previously, then I ordered breakfast.

"I thought you'd like to have this," I said, and then asked if he still had the Shelby.

"Yup" is all he said.

I didn't say anything more.

About a week later, I went back to Bob's diner for lunch. I ordered a cheeseburger and fries. This time Bob came out to my booth and sat with me. We spoke for a while about his racing photos on the wall.

"Tom, I really appreciate the book," he said. "Say, you're always asking about the Shelby. Would you like to see it?"

"Oh yeah," I said.

Within minutes, I was a passenger in his minivan as we apexed turns in the neighborhood just a few blocks away. In the yard behind a small brick house sat the sorry-looking lime gold Shelby, covered with leaves and pine needles, looking forgotten.

Bob unlocked the door. I sat inside. The seats had mildewed, but the car was surprisingly correct and complete. And it only had thirty-four thousand miles on the odometer. The automatic-equipped car was like a time capsule; even the exhaust system was original. So were the heater hoses and all the clamps. In fact, the original tags on the carburetor and the distributor were still in place.

"Want to hear it run?" Bob asked.

I had to catch my breath; you mean to say that a car that has been off the road since 1980 still runs?

"I had a mechanic buddy of mine go through it and get it running," he said. Clearly he had given thought to selling the car, and I just happened to be in the right place at the right time.

Fortunately, that mechanic didn't remove the original parts, as is often done with restored collector cars. Bob jumped behind the wheel, and she fired right up. The car ran well, although loudly, because time and corrosion were parting out the original exhaust system.

As the car sat there idling, Bob told me the story of buying the car from Hickory Ford in North Carolina for his wife to drive to her job at the real estate office. That's why it had an automatic. And that's why I believed he bought it new.

Odds were good that since it was his wife's car, it was not driven as hard as a typical "guy-owned" muscle car would have been back in the 1970s.

He asked me how much I'd offer him for the car. I said I'd like to come back the next week with Jim, look the car over really closely, and then be prepared to make an offer.

Jim is a nut for originality. The following week, we came armed with Jim's parts books and combed over the car. It was real, it was low mileage, and it was possibly one of the most-original Shelbys in existence. Even the original Goodyear Sports Car Special spare tire was still in the trunk, probably still inflated with the original 1967 air.

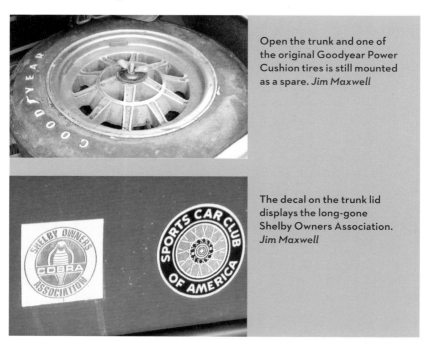

Open the trunk and one of the original Goodyear Power Cushion tires is still mounted as a spare. *Jim Maxwell*

The decal on the trunk lid displays the long-gone Shelby Owners Association. *Jim Maxwell*

But first, we ordered cheeseburgers and fries from Bob's diner.

Making an offer was going to be tricky business. Sure, we would like to own the car for the least amount of money possible, but I didn't want to low-ball Bob, who had become a friend. I'm sure that the scores of other folks who hounded him over the years tried to "steal" it.

We came up with a fair market value of the car of $65,000; not free, but it was an amount we thought both Bob and we could live with.

"Boys, you just bought yourself a car!" he said.

The following week, when we went to retrieve our new acquisition, Bob had discovered two more of the original tires that came on the car and proudly presented them to us.

We had the car looked over by Walt Pierce of Huntersville, North Carolina, who specializes in maintaining original Ford performance cars. He tuned the car, rebuilt the brake hydraulics, and changed all the fluids. The Shelby runs great, although still loudly because we refuse to change the original exhaust system.

We drove the GT500 to the Shelby National Convention at Virginia International Raceway during the summer of 2006, and it was a hit. There, among hundreds of beautifully restored Shelbys and Cobras, sat our GT500 rat, and boy, did people love it. Judges combed over the car, looking for the multitude of untouched details that every Shelby came with new.

"Please, never restore this car" was a theme Jim and I heard over and over. "Save it as a reference for all the other restored '67 GT500s."

Since that time, the car has been displayed at Lowe's Motor Speedway at AutoFair, next to several restored Shelbys to highlight the newly introduced GT500. Craig Jackson, of the Barrett-Jackson Auction, was at AutoFair that week appraising cars for a television special that would air before his 2007 auction.

Craig loved the car.

"Don't restore this car," he said.

It seemed that we really had a unique set of wheels on our hands.

While at AutoFair, a gentleman named Jim Adams introduced himself and said that he had actually purchased the lime gold Shelby new in 1967.

"I worked in the dealership body shop, and a customer ordered this car," he said. "But when the car came in, the customer decided he didn't want it. So I bought it and owned it for two years. When I sold it, it only had twelve hundred miles on it."

How did Adams identify the car?

"The car came without stripes, so I painted those black stripes right in the dealership body shop. I could tell my stripes anywhere."

THE SUPERBIRD IN THE BUSHES

Barry Lee first heard about the Superbird from an unreliable source. After all, the guy had already snookered Lee out of two Plymouth 'Cudas that he had pursued on eBay.

"This guy would deal in muscle cars," said Lee, a motorcycle dealer near Jacksonville, Florida. "But he sold the two 'Cudas from under me after I had committed to them."

Lee's business was booming, and this allowed him to pursue the Mopar muscle cars he had loved since he was a kid. He was into Chrysler's big-block 'Cudas, Super Bees, and Challengers. But his dream was to someday own either a long-snouted, big-winged Plymouth Superbird or its similarly styled cousin, the Dodge Daytona.

These cars were built with one purpose in mind: to win NASCAR races. The slippery nose and tall tail helped these cars go fast and stay planted, earning wins for drivers such as Richard Petty, Buddy Baker, and Bobby Allison. But the street versions were never winners in the showroom. The odd-looking vehicles were sold to the public for homologation purposes only; NASCAR rules required that a certain number of street versions be built for any model a manufacturer wanted to race on the stock car circuit.

Lee's not-so-dependable contact must have had a change of heart, because he phoned Lee to tell him about a Superbird he heard about in Alabama.

"He told me something about the car having been owned by a guy who was missing in action in Vietnam, and it had been sitting since 1975," Lee

Find the hidden Superbird! At first, Barry Lee didn't see the Superbird he had heard about in an Alabama yard. It had been parked behind a house for nearly thirty years, and eventually the hedge grew up around it. *Barry Lee*

said. "He gave me an address and only asked for a finder's fee if I purchased the car."

Fair enough, Lee thought, and he made plans to see the winged Plymouth.

"Alabama was more than four hours from my home, and my wife wasn't in the mood to take a long drive," he said. "But I told her I'd take her to Biloxi, Mississippi, for some gambling over Christmas if we could stop in Alabama on the way. She was all for it."

When Lee pulled up to the house, he thought the wheeler-dealer Mopar salesman had pulled another fast one on him. The property was overgrown, the house was abandoned, and the roof had collapsed. Lee walked around the yard and looked at a couple of old trucks and cars that were lying about, but there was nothing exciting. Then his wife noticed a small piece of bright orange inside the hedge. Lee pushed away the branches and discovered the car of his dreams: a 1970 Plymouth Superbird that had actually become part of the hedge!

Lee found out who owned the house and called the phone number.

"When I called and asked about the car, they hung up the phone on me," he said.

The elderly owner, Frank Moran, whose wife was in a nursing home, lived nearby with his daughter.

"So then I had my wife call, and she and Frank were having a nice conversation until she mentioned the Plymouth. Then he hung up on her too."

The Lees went on to Biloxi and had an enjoyable holiday and decided to pursue the Superbird later.

Lee gives his wife full credit for coming up with a plan on acquiring the Plymouth. Call it woman's intuition, but she suggested that they simply write a letter that expressed their desire to buy the car. What did he have to lose?

It was several weeks after their Alabama trip that Lee wrote the letter to both the elderly Frank Moran and his daughter. In it, he said he'd like to restore the car—to remove it from the elements that were destroying it—and that Moran could keep the title. It was quite a charitable offer, but it went unanswered.

"It was out of my hands," Lee said. And at least a year went by before he received a surprise phone call.

"Hello, Barry? This is George Proux, Frank Moran's son-in-law," the caller announced. Lee's heart began racing. "Frank fell and is in the hospital. I have power of attorney, and I had all the cars hauled off before I found your letter. I figured I should give you a call and let you know that the Plymouth you are interested in is sitting at my house in Jacksonville, Florida."

Only about fifteen minutes from Lee's house!

Proux was a muscle car enthusiast. In fact, when he first married Moran's daughter, he had tried to purchase the Superbird from Moran, but he was denied. With Moran's declining health, Proux and his son hauled the car to their Florida home in the hopes of restoring it. But Lee hoped they would consider selling it, because the Superbird's restoration was more than an average hobby restorer could handle.

Proux said that a museum in Alabama had been calling about acquiring the car, but he wanted to give Lee the first opportunity because the letter he had written was so sincere.

"I went over and looked at the car and we talked," Lee said. "At the time, I was driving a very nice, 1970 factory big-block lime green Road Runner."

Lee and Proux traded.

"He got what he wanted and I got what I wanted," said Lee, very pleased with the transaction.

Lee's barn find is equipped with a numbers-matching 440-cubic-inch engine, column-mounted automatic transmission, and bench seat. It still has its original bias-ply Goodyear Wide Oval tires mounted on rally wheels. It was one of 1,920 Superbirds manufactured.

It was only after he acquired the car that Lee was finally able to meet Frank Moran and learn of the car's history.

"Frank was a super-nice guy; he was in a walker when I met him," Lee said.

Moran had traded a boat for the Superbird in 1974. He drove it but didn't enjoy being followed by people who wanted to talk to him about the car. Apparently, Moran once ran off someone inquiring about the car with a shotgun.

"He was kind of a private guy," Lee said.

Finally, having driven it less than one thousand miles and fed up with the notoriety the car was bringing him, he pulled the car out of sight and parked it behind his house. Eventually, the hedge slowly engulfed the orange car so that it wasn't visible even to someone standing next to it. That's where Lee first spotted the car. Unfortunately, the time since he first saw the car had taken its toll on the Superbird's condition.

A hurricane that took landfall in Pensacola in 2004 blew down a tree, which broke out the back window and dented the roof and rear quarter panel. Then thieves had made off with many of the car's unique parts, such as the rear wing, hood, radio, front fender scoops, and radiator.

"I was surprised at the car's poor condition when I saw it in Jacksonville," Lee said.

Luckily, Lee came across a "clone" Superbird, from which he was able to buy replacements for many of the stolen metal and fiberglass pieces. However, he still needed the rear window—which is unique to the Superbird and extremely rare. Incredibly, Lee was able to locate a parts vendor in Myrtle Beach, South Carolina, who had a brand-new rear window for the car still in the original carton.

"I finally have my dream car," Lee said. "This car is a keeper."

"It will get a full rotisserie restoration and be the most serious restoration I've ever done. Because of the moist, salty, and humid environment the car had lived in for so many years, the floors, trunk, frame rails, and some of the firewall need to be replaced."

But first, Lee is completing the restoration of a 1969 Super Bee. Then a 1969 Camaro Convertible. Then a 1971 'Cuda.

Then comes the Superbird.

"I owe it to my wife, whose idea of a letter worked," he said. "Persistence paid off."

"When it's restored, I think it will be the lowest-mileage Superbird in the world."

THE MOB GTO

Lake Placid, New York, is a small town tucked away in the Adirondack Mountains about one hundred miles south of the Canadian border. It's the type of area where people know each other's business, and secrets are rare.

Over twenty years ago, Rob Bugbee chose this community as his new home, chucking the pressures of his ABC Sports job to pursue his passion for old cars. Bugbee opened Alpine Restorations, which specializes in making neglected muscle cars look new.

You'd imagine that as the owner of an automotive restoration business in this tiny community, Bugbee would know about every car for miles around. Not necessarily.

As my friend Bill Warner knows all too well, sometimes terrific cars can be discovered—or not discovered—just blocks away from your own home. And all car collectors can tell stories of losing a terrific car that was right under their nose.

Bugbee is the third owner of a 1968 Pontiac GTO convertible that had been sitting about one mile from his house in Wilmington, New York, for more than thirty years. He later found he was one of the few people who didn't know about the car.

"A friend of mine called and said he was moving, and he had to get rid of this old muscle car in his garage," Bugbee said. "He rented a garage storage spot to this guy about thirty years earlier, but the guy never paid any rent and never picked it up, so finally he just had to find a new home for it."

Rob Bugbee followed up on a lead about an old GTO in a garage near his Lake Placid, New York, home. After he purchased and inspected it, he discovered that the highly optioned convertible, formerly owned by a mobster, was perhaps the rarest GTO in existence. *Rob Bugbee*

"So I went down there, and the car was surrounded with old bicycles and other junk."

Thankfully, the car was covered and sitting on jack stands.

"I said to myself, 'Wow, it's a convertible, and it's got a four speed,'" he said.

But Bugbee didn't want to pay the amount being asked for the car, so he waited about six weeks before he wheeled and dealed with his friend for the best price.

Bugbee won't say how much he paid for the car in 2003 but said it was less than the $5,037.14 list price that the car sold for when new.

"It was dirt cheap," he said. "I didn't realize what it was. I thought I'd just fix it up and flip it for a profit."

But when Bugbee got the car back to his shop and began cleaning it up, he became interested in some of the markings and codes under the hood.

"I'm looking at the production codes, and it said Ram Air II, so I called a friend of mine in Michigan who really knows Pontiacs," he said. "I gave him all the codes, and he wasn't very familiar with them, so he told me he'd call me back.

"When he called, he said, 'I hope you're sitting down, because you just bought the rarest GTO on Earth!' I'm looking at the phone and saying, 'You've got to be kidding me.'"

Bugbee said that this car had been casually for sale for about twenty years.

"Every car guy in the area had heard about it, and I was the last one to hear about it," he said. "But since the rumors were that the car had a blown engine and a blown rear, nobody was interested."

The car, VIN number 242678B130848, had been ordered in 1968 with twenty-five options, which was very unusual—and expensive—in those days. The original Long Island owner is rumored to have been connected with the mob. But this mobster had good taste in cars. He ordered the black-on-black with gold interior convertible from Triangle Pontiac in Queens with virtually every option available.

The GTO's Protect-O-Plate specifications list shows that the car is equipped with engine code XS, which designates a 400-cubic-inch, 360-horsepower Ram Air engine. When ordered with the manual transmission, the compression ratio was an aggressive 10.75:1. Bugbee said that power output is above the engine's 366 rated horsepower.

"It's probably closer to four hundred twenty-five horsepower if you do the math," he said. "Basically, the car was built with a detuned racing engine. These cars aren't very pleasant to drive around town; they don't make good grocery getters."

Bugbee discovered that the car's 4.33 rear-end ratio had been damaged sometime in its life. Since a timing slip from New York National Speedway was discovered in the glove box, a blown rear didn't surprise him. But the good news is that Bugbee located a correct ZL-code 4.33 rear that had been sitting on a collector's shelf for eighteen years.

Some of the other options on the car include a hood-mounted tach, power disc brakes, Rally II Wheels, a handling package, an AM/FM radio, power windows, a power antenna, a remote trunk release, a wood steering wheel and shift knob, a lighted ignition switch, an under-hood lamp, a trunk lamp, console, a vanity mirror, door edge guards, hidden headlights, cornering lamps, exhaust tips, and a spare tire cover.

"No dealer would have ordered that many options," Bugbee said. "They all add up to sixteen hundred dollars, which was a huge amount for 1968."

At some point, the original owner must have tired of owning his car, so he passed it to the second owner, who purchased it with forty-eight thousand miles on the clock. Owner number two put it into long-term storage with about fifty-two thousand miles on it, which is what the odometer still reads.

Bugbee brought the car back to his shop and quickly got it running, even with thirty-year-old fuel in the tank. He discovered that the car was in amazing condition without a speck of rust.

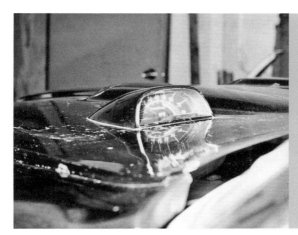

The 1968 Ram Air II car was equipped with twenty-five factory options, including this rare hood-mounted tachometer. *Rob Bugbee*

Even though Bugbee is a dyed-in-the-wool Chevy guy, he quickly learned all he could about Pontiacs.

"There is only one other four-speed convertible like mine, but it has only three or four options," he said. "And there is an automatic convertible that is known as well. There were six or eight convertibles originally built with the Ram Air II engine and about two hundred forty-three hardtops.

"Everyone has been looking for Judge convertibles, but for real Pontiac collectors, my car is the one missing from all the big collections."

Since purchasing the GTO, Bugbee has simply cleaned up the car, and he has no plans to restore it. In 2003, he trailered the car to Pontiac, Michigan, for the twenty-fifth GTO Association of America National Convention. He brought it there simply to show fellow enthusiasts what he had found, but he came away with some surprising hardware.

"The car won Best of Concourse Factory Original, the Dualgate Award, and the Silver Concourse Award," he said.

"I can't tell you how many guys have come up to me and said I stole the GTO," Bugbee said. "This is from guys who knew about the car before I did.

"All I can say is that they didn't do their homework, and I did."

THE GREATEST BARN FIND STORY EVER TOLD

Larry Fisette is not a bragger. He's a solid Midwesterner with solid Midwestern values, which includes not boasting about your deeds. Yet for those of us who dream of stumbling across the ultimate barn find before our time runs out, sit down and hold on as you read his story.

Fisette owns a modest auto repair shop and restoration business in De Pere, Wisconsin—not exactly the focal point of the antique car world. If you go to his website (www.depereautocenter.com), you'll see some of the special interest cars he sells. But you'll only find a small reference of the "find" that once had the old car world buzzing and consumed nearly one year of his life.

"I've been chasing old cars my whole life," Fisette said. "I'm as big an old car guy as you can be."

As an old car aficionado, Fisette would frequent car shows and flea markets. Occasionally at these shows, he would see a gentleman named Don Schlag.

"I had heard of this guy since I moved here in 1969," said Fisette, whose own collection includes a Crosley Hot Shot and a 1959 fuel-injected Impala. "I'd see him at swap meets and we'd say 'Hi,' but not much beyond that."

But Fisette had heard from fellow enthusiasts that the never-married Schlag dedicated his life to scrounging parts. He was, in fact, a mega-collector who had a passion for big-block and high-performance Chevrolet products, and he had quite a stash hidden from public view.

Schlag began to collect high-performance cars and parts many years ago. At first, he would stash the parts in his home garage. When the garage began brimming with parts, he started to move parts into the house. As his passion for collecting grew beyond the house, he used the back of his father's John Deere and implement dealership—Green Bay Equipment—to store the cars and parts he was constantly dragging home. He even made an annual month-long trip to California, and he towed a box trailer behind his motorhome so that he could bring home his purchases.

"Don started buying out old inventory at Chevy dealerships in this area, then he started traveling west every year," Fisette said.

Schlag also developed quite a business during the fuel crisis in the 1970s when the public had no appetite for big-block, gas-guzzling cars stacking up on Chevy dealership lots. Schlag would pick up the big-block cars from the dealerships and bring them to his father's dealership, where he would pull the 427- or 454-cubic-inch engines and substitute them for more fuel-efficient small-block engines. He would then keep the larger engine and charge the dealership $100 to boot!

What drove Schlag to collect these items—during a time when the public had no stomach for such machines—is indeed curious. Was he a "hoarder" of these curious high-horsepower components, or did he in fact suspect that one day the public would again salivate over everything related to the muscle car era?

Schlag wasn't an exclusive parts collector; he occasionally bought cars as well. Fisette once heard that Schlag bought an authentic Yenko Camaro for $1,250 in 1970.

"I didn't have twelve hundred and fifty dollars for any car that my wife couldn't drive in 1970," Fisette said.

Nobody was quite sure of what cars Schlag had because he was so reclusive.

Two events led to Schlag's reclusiveness: his father died in the early 1970s and the family's retail dealership was liquidated, and a fellow enthusiast stole a rare part from Schlag's collection.

Schlag began moving his cars and parts into forty-eight-foot trailers, and when each trailer was full, he would weld up the doors and back another trailer directly against the doors, making them impossible to open.

He even stopped driving his prized Corvettes when one was once keyed in a parking lot. He stored those, too, but only after he performed an odd transplant on each. Schlag would swap the engines from car to car, thereby taking the correct numbers-matching engines out of each car. It is believed that Schlag performed this ritual in an effort to make the cars less desirable to thieves.

Cars were also parked nose to tail in the welded-shut trailers. Here is one of the rarest cars in the purchase, an authentic 1969 Yenko Camaro. *Larry Fisette*

One day the rumor that Don Schlag had died began circulating among enthusiasts.

"I heard that he died, so I called his sister and left a message," Fisette said. "I said that I would like to buy the entire collection and then properly manage a liquidation sale.

"I said I would only call once and leave a message. I had given up hope when about four months later I was driving back from our cabin and I received a call from Don's sister. She said she and her children had done a background check on me, and that I was chosen to buy the collection, that I was the one she trusted."

Fisette had no idea what he had committed to. He met the sister, Joanne Stepien, at her deceased brother's house, and they started to clear out the garage. The contents included two Corvettes in addition to loads of parts. After finishing with the garage, they moved on to the closets, the dining room, the kitchen, and the bathrooms. He made an offer for those parts and felt quite satisfied with his good fortune.

"When we thought we had the house completely cleaned out, we made one more sweep through and found a couple more items," Fisette said. "A set of Ed Pink cylinder heads and a fuel injection unit for a 1957 Pontiac."

Then the sister asked if he'd like to start on the rest of the collection.

There was more?

Lots more. Twenty-one tractor-trailer loads more.

"We emptied out the first trailer and spread the items across a warehouse floor," Fisette said. "Stepien's son and I each came up with the value of each trailer. They were very, very fair. It was a trusting deal on both sides."

The first trailer contained two 1970 LS-6 Chevelles parked nose to tail. One was a gold, four-speed bench seat car, and the other was an automatic bucket-seat model. Then he stumbled on the aforementioned 1969 Yenko Camaro. A total of fourteen cars were uncovered, including two fuel-injected 1957 Corvettes, a 1963 split-window Corvette coupe, a 1964 fuel-injected Corvette roadster, a 1967 435-horsepower Corvette roadster, a 1967 RS/SS Camaro, and a 1972 Z/28 Camaro.

To list the tens of thousands of parts that Fisette purchased from the locked trailers would take up half this book, but highlights include an experimental fuel injection for a big-block Chevy, brand-new factory side exhausts for Corvettes, a cast-iron COPO 427 engine block, new knock-off Corvette wheels, and even a Yenko hubcap. Fifty-five-gallon drums were filled with crankshafts and performance cylinder heads.

Fisette unearthed more than 150 high-performance engines, including six 1969 Z/28 DZ 302 engines, complete down to the breather.

When word of Fisette's discovery began circulating among enthusiasts, the phone at De Pere Auto Center started ringing off the hook. It was all he and his staff could do just to answer the phone from opening to closing each day.

"We had our four phone lines lit for ten straight days," he said. "We could hardly conduct business."

"On one day, I had two hundred and fifty cars in my parking lot and five hundred people walking around the warehouse I rented, and they all wanted something that I had."

One day, Fisette hauled seven car loads of people from the airport to the fourteen-thousand-square-foot warehouse. In his sincere Midwestern way, he transported the visitors, made hotel reservations, and suggested restaurants.

Was it tiring for Fisette? Hardly.

"I hated to go to bed and couldn't wait to wake up," he said. "I now have friends from all over the country that I'd like to have a beer with."

He had offers coming in from all over the country and around the world. He considered splitting up the collection, which could have become a full-time career selling the pieces on eBay, but decided against it.

"I'm sixty-six years old," he said. "It would have taken me ten years to sell everything. I don't have that much time. But if I were younger, I would have kept everything. I would have restored every car and sold every part individually. It interfered with our regular business because all the parts and cars were a business in itself."

Here a 1963 Corvette Stingray split-window coupe is pushed from its trailer tomb. *Larry Fisette*

In the end, Fisette chose to sell the entire collection to one individual, collector Scott Milestone of Maryland, who already owns a sizable car collection. Fisette sold every single part, down to the last pushrod.

"The buyer had five guys loading the parts into trailers nine hours a day, and it took two weeks. You have no idea how much there was," he said.

"As the truck was pulling out, I saw that a pushrod we used to hold an electrical cord was still in place. I ran outside and gave it to them. I promised I'd sell him everything."

Milestone feels privileged and lucky to have been chosen as the next caretaker of the immense muscle car find.

"Not many people would have been in the position to buy the entire collection," said Milestone, who has purchased several large collections over the years. "Over time, I'll begin breaking up the parts and cars and selling them."

Fisette wishes Milestone well.

"I hope he does as well as I did when he sells the collection because he deserves it," he said.

After being cleaned up, eight of the fourteen cars were removed from Schlag's trailers. Collectors flew from around the country to view the stash that Fisette had acquired. *Larry Fisette*

During the nearly one year of living with one of the largest Chevy barn finds in history, Fisette feels he learned something about Don Schlag.

"I kind of got into his skin," Fisette said. "He had to have been a visionary.

"I think he had a grand plan to one day have a warehouse and be able to see all his stuff lined up. But he died before he could get that accomplished."

Fisette knows exactly the feeling. When he had the thousands and thousands of parts lined up in two rented warehouses—along with the fourteen rare cars—he had an odd feeling of power and accomplishment.

Fisette has had many memorable experiences in the old car business, like the time entertainer Jay Leno—who was performing at a nearby casino—stopped in De Pere Auto Center to look at a supercharged Kaiser that was sitting on the lot. That chance visit began a friendship that continues today.

But he said nothing comes close to the barn find.

Did Fisette have a favorite car or a favorite part that he would have liked to have kept?

"The Yenko Camaro was my favorite car," he said. "I had an offer of two hundred thousand dollars for that car alone. But I also fell in love with some of the rare parts: big brakes for solid-axle Corvettes, for instance, which were installed on cars that were built for racing. These had metallic linings, and when the cars were used on the street, they didn't work well, so they were usually taken off and discarded. A set of those are probably worth twenty-five thousand to thirty thousand dollars.

Once Fisette removed, inventoried, and stored the parts in a rented warehouse, the enormity of the purchase became apparent. More than 150 engines and rare factory fuel injection units were included. *Larry Fisette*

"Then there were all the fuel-injection units, factory aluminum cylinder heads, and big gas tanks for 1960 Corvettes. There were all sorts of parts you couldn't buy, no matter how much money you had."

These days, life is much calmer. No more fielding phone calls from around the world and no more runs to the airport to pick up potential buyers. Fisette is back to repairing cars and hunting for more hidden treasure.

He has spoken to a number of people about liquidating their collections, but most he's not interested in.

"These days, nobody wants a trailer of Model A Ford parts," he said.

But he is excited about another pending deal.

"I've been working on it for six months," he said. "If it happens, the thirty-five-to forty-car collection and parts will surpass the Schlag deal."

But Fisette is not pushing. He's made his one phone call and will sit back and wait. It's what Midwesterners do.

THE FATHER & SON HUNTING TEAM

Don and Keith Isley have the perfect father-and-son hobby: searching for old cars. The two have developed an eye for seeing cars that are virtually invisible to most enthusiasts.

Take the Corvette discovered by son Keith as the family was driving home to Greensboro, North Carolina, from a vacation in Myrtle Beach, South Carolina, back in the mid-2000s.

"We had been driving for four or five hours," said Keith. That's when he said to his father, "Stop!"

Father Don thought something was the matter, so he quickly came to a stop.

"What's the matter?" he asked his son.

"There's a 1970 Dodge Challenger back there."

So, as they had done so many times before, Don turned around the family car and drove back to the Challenger on the side of the road. All this happened without waking up a sleeping Mrs. Isley in the back seat.

The two enthusiasts spoke to the car's owner for thirty to forty minutes. The car wasn't for sale, so they kept driving up the road.

One mile later, Keith yelled, "Stop!"

"Now what?" asked Don.

"I saw something in an old garage," answered Keith. "I think it might have been James Dean's Porsche." Keith, at the time twelve years old, certainly had a robust imagination.

"No more stopping, we need to get home," said Don, who had more than an hour left to drive before they pulled in their driveway. Mrs. Isley still hadn't woken from her sleep.

Keith never forgot that car in the garage. It was more than a hundred feet off the road, surrounded by trees and partially blocked from view by cardboard boxes and other trash.

Six months later, again returning from a weekend at Myrtle Beach, he remembered the garage and this time convinced his dad to stop.

Instead of James Dean's Porsche 550 Spyder, the car-hunting duo found an old Corvette parked in the open garage. It was the ideal barn find.

"We knocked on the door of the house, but nobody was home," said Don, forty-eight. "So I left a business card in his mailbox with a note and kept driving toward home."

The Isleys never heard from the Corvette's owner, so Don did an Internet search for the name on the mailbox. Calling the phone number, he spoke to the woman who answered.

"Oh, that car belongs to my son," she said. "His number is unlisted, but I'll give it to you."

The next phone call began a relationship that continues today.

The car belonged to Bill McKinnon, who purchased the 1960 Corvette as a used car in 1967 for $1,200. "I was nineteen or twenty years old and found it on a used car lot in Asheboro [North Carolina]. There were two Corvettes on the lot, a customized one and this one, which was original. I decided the original one looked better, so I bought it. The car had about sixty thousand miles on it when I bought it."

It was McKinnon's everyday car from 1967 until the mid-1980s, when he parked it in his garage with about 120,000 miles on the odometer.

"We offered to buy the car from Bill, but it wasn't for sale," Don said. "Then we offered to take the car out of his garage, clean the car and the garage, and install a proper garage door, but he said it could stay there just fine.

"So I asked him if we could stop by and visit next time we drove by, and Bill said, 'Sure.'"

The Isleys also offered to bring the Corvette to a warehouse his brother owned in Greensboro for secure storage. They even offered to get the car running and go through the mechanics, but McKinnon wasn't interested.

On one of the family's biannual trips to Myrtle Beach, Don and Keith stopped at McKinnon's and gave him a gift: a copy of my book, *The Hemi in the Barn*. Inside they wrote a nice message and their name and phone number.

After removing the rubbish, this is what they found. Bill McKinnon, who has owned the car since 1967, wasn't interested in selling, but said that he enjoyed meeting Keith and his father, Don, and that they could come visit any time they liked. *Tom Cotter*

"Our fingers are still crossed that one day we'll get that phone call from Bill that he's ready to sell us the car," Don said.

Buying a Collector's Collection

The Isley boys, father Don and son Keith, have it figured out. Rather than search for one interesting car here and another there, they search out older car collectors who often have several cars in the garage or in the "lower forty."

Here's how they lucked onto a multiple gold mine:

"We were riding down the road one day and went past an old homestead," Don said. "We had driven past the place many times, but this time the garage door was open, and inside we saw a 1969 Camaro.

"A nice older gentleman spoke to us for a long time. It turns out he was a retired engineer from AT&T in Burlington, North Carolina, near Elon, the town where we lived at the time. For many years, he would buy an interesting car, use it for a while, then put it up."

The gentleman had good taste; inside the garage and various carports that had not been visible from the road sat a 1969 Corvette, 1965 Mustang convertible, 1956 Ford Thunderbird, 1930 Model A Tudor, and two 1950 Fords, a coupe and a convertible.

Outside were many, many more vehicles. Behind the garage sat three motor homes, three boats, several later Thunderbirds, a couple of Cougars, and some 1970s Camaros.

In what resembled an apple orchard toward the back of his property sat at least twenty more cars that, according to Isley, had been there for twenty or more years.

Included in that group were Cadillacs, Mercurys, Rancheros, some tractors, and a fairly nice 1949 Ford pickup.

"He had a compressor and some tools in a back garage," Isley said. "It seemed he liked to tinker.

"He showed us everything and enjoyed spending time with us. We were mostly interested in the Camaro for Keith, but he said he could never sell that car. 'My wife would kill me.'"

They didn't know it at the time, but this would be the last time they would speak with the gentleman.

Don and Keith said thank you and departed. They waited six months, called the house, and spoke to the man's wife.

"Yeah, I know he spoke to someone and showed you his cars, but nothing is ever going to be for sale," she said.

They waited six months and then called, and the wife told them the same thing.

Six months later when Don called, there was no answer. He found out through a man in town that the family had moved to Florida and actually sold the property but retained lifetime rights to keep the cars parked there.

Six more months and Don searched for the couple in Florida through the Internet. He wrote an email letter offering to help the couple get the cars running.

"We never heard from them," said Don.

The town of Burlington is in Alamance County. At the time, a new ordinance was passed that restricted property owners to no more than two unregistered cars visible from the road, and they had to be covered.

"When we made our semiannual phone call, the wife said that she knew of the new restriction, and that, 'We'll have to come up there to straighten it out,'" said Isley. "But we didn't hear from her again."

Once when Don and Keith were traveling to the 24 Hour Race at Daytona, they attempted to visit the couple in nearby Astor, Florida, near Deland on the St. John's River. But as usual, they left a message and never received a reply.

"We're about four and one half years into this relationship at this point, and we were still going nowhere," said Don. Or so he thought.

"The wife called and told us her son, who lived in Greensboro, wanted to talk to us. It turns out that the older gentleman had Alzheimer's disease and was unable to manage his affairs.

"She told us that the man who bought their Burlington property had paid them additional money so he could begin construction of a subdivision immediately, so the cars had to go."

When Don and Keith spoke to the son, he asked them to make a list of the cars they were interested in and how much they were willing to pay. Their list included the 1956 Thunderbird, the two 1950 Fords, the 1949 Ford pickup, and two Cougars. And of course, the Camaro.

"The son met us over there and we made him an offer on each car," he said. "He told us that his stepfather had purchased the '56 T-Bird in 1958 from Atwater Ford, the local Burlington Ford agency on Main Street. It had only fifty-six thousand four hundred miles on it.

"It was in nice condition even though the roof in the garage leaked on the car every time it rained.

"He told us he wanted a little more money than we offered him for the Thunderbird, but once we upped that, he agreed to sell us everything except the Camaro, which was a four-speed RS/SS. That car was given to him by his stepdad."

Finally, by March 2009, Isley was able to buy the collection's most desirable cars.

Out of the blue soon after the transaction, Don received a phone call from a man in Burlington. "I heard you bought a few of those old cars," he said. "I've been trying to buy that 1950 Ford convertible from him for twenty years, but that old bastard wouldn't sell it. I'd like to buy it from you if you're interested."

"So I decided to sell the Ford to him," said Don. "He bought it and has done a nice job on it.

"Funny thing was, when we started dragging cars out of there, lots of people would stop by there and tell us they'd been trying to buy these cars for thirty-five years.

"I sold the '49 Ford pickup to one guy who stopped by as we were loading up cars on trailers."

While the Isleys were loading up their stash, other collectors who had purchased cars from the son were also loading up cars. According to Don, one man bought all the Falcons and Rancheros, another bought all the pickup trucks.

"People were lined up there all day Saturday," said Don.

Of all the people who had attempted to purchase the collection of cars, it was Don and Keith Isley who had the patience and perseverance to see it through.

What a great gift a father can pass onto his son.

THE CORNFIELD
HEMI 'CUDA

Greg Peterson drove a yellow Corvair Spyder convertible during his high school years. He graduated with honors, and his proud father and grandfather wanted to send Greg off to engineering school driving a brand-new car.

Greg didn't mind his Corvair, which handled well and was reliable, but both his dad and granddad were car enthusiasts. They wanted to reward him for doing so well in school with something a little sportier.

Greg was given a choice of either a new Corvette or a Plymouth Hemi 'Cuda. In 1970, the seventeen-year-old, his father, and his grandfather walked into Carlson Motor Sales in Morris, Illinois, to order the 'Cuda. The son may have been reluctant to give up his Corvair, but his father was more than prepared to place the order for him. Mr. Peterson had studied the sales brochure well, and when they sat down with the salesman, he rattled off the list of options he desired: a 426 Hemi engine, four-speed transmission, Trac-Pac 3:54 Dana 60 rear end, TorRed paint, black leather bucket seats, power steering, power brakes, power windows, fifteen-by-seven-inch Rallye Wheels, AM/FM radio with rear speaker, Rallye dash gauges, three-spoke wood steering wheel, dual-painted Sport Mirrors, painted grille, and rear window defroster.

The salesman calculated a retail price, but the three shrewd farmers sitting in front of him haggled fiercely. When a fair price was agreed upon, the salesman told them that he dropped the price only because he always wanted to sell a Hemi car.

Open wide and say . . . vroom! This time-capsule Hemi 'Cuda hadn't seen daylight since 1974, nearly 33 years. According to Scott Smith, who authenticated the car, it is perhaps the most original Hemi 'Cuda in existence. *Scott Smith*

On January 30, 1971, Greg received a call that his new car had arrived and it was ready to be picked up. Once he drove it home, he realized two things about his new car: one was that it was a handful to drive compared to his Corvair and the other was that fender lip moldings were only installed on the driver's side of the 'Cuda.

That was curious, because he had not even ordered fender moldings. The embarrassed dealer couldn't explain the mishap. He installed the same moldings on the passenger side and sent young Greg down the road, but not before giving him a small paper packet of special valve stem extensions that were required with the Rallye Wheels. Greg installed those extensions when he got home and saved the original short extensions in the packet and placed it inside the center console.

Greg didn't really enjoy driving his new car. He found it irritating that it was hard to take off from a stop sign without spinning the rear tires. His high school yearbook had a photo of Greg and his 'Cuda with a handwritten sign in the rear window that read "Chevy Eater," but he was no speed demon. During his high school and college years, he never received a speeding ticket, had an accident, or even had a flat tire.

Preferring his Corvair's less aggressive nature, Greg drove the 'Cuda sparingly, accumulating only 11,318 miles before parking it in his family's barn in 1974.

Fast forward more than three decades: During the summer of 2006, Scott Smith was surfing the web when he came across a post that someone wanted to get his 'Cuda's carburetors rebuilt. Smith, who restores Mopar muscle cars and rebuilds components, responded with an email but didn't think much more about it.

The next day, Smith received a phone call from the gentleman who posted the request. "He told me the carbs were for his '71 Hemi 'Cuda, which didn't surprise me too much because of all the clones out there," Smith said.

"I asked him if the carburetors were complete, and the caller said yes, that they had only eleven thousand miles on them. He said he hadn't started the car since 1974."

The original tires, including the valve stem extensions, still hold 1974 air! *Scott Smith*

The phone call was, of course, from Greg Petersen. He wanted to refresh the car that had been sitting in the barn since the mid-1970s.

"Greg told me his barber, who had a generic photo of a Hemi 'Cuda hanging on the wall in his shop, one day mentioned to him, 'Too bad you still don't have your old 'Cuda,' to which Greg answered, 'Yes, I do.'

"Then the barber said, 'Oh, it probably needs a lot of restoration,' to which Greg responded, 'No, it's just like I parked it.'"

Greg had also seen the televised Barrett-Jackson auction and saw a similar car to his sell for about $1 million.

"He told me he bought it new but parked it after driving it after just a few years," Smith said. "I asked him to please not do anything to the car because I wanted to see it with my own eyes before any work was done."

Travel arrangements were quickly made, and soon Smith was on a flight from Washington to Chicago to document this very rare survivor.

When Smith arrived in Chicago, he had no idea what to expect. Was the story real? Was it a clone? As he pulled his rental car up to the storage barn in the middle of a cornfield, he expected to see a tractor or some other farm implement inside. Instead, he faced the most original 1971 Hemi 'Cuda on the planet, a time capsule that had not seen the light of day in thirty-three years.

"The car had been parked on a packed gravel and dirt floor," Smith said.

"After all the years, the tires, which still had 1974 air in them, had sunken about one inch into the ground. We pushed it outside and gave it a gentle sponge bath. Then I photographed the heck out of it."

How many times have you driven past a farm and wondered what was sitting behind the barn doors? Ninety-nine percent of the time, it's just an old tractor or a pickup truck at best. But this particular barn near Morris, Illinois, had a special vehicle inside, and, yup, it was powered by a Hemi. *Scott Smith*

Peterson had never washed under the hood, so all the original markings and details were still intact.

Smith was treated to a virgin example of a Hemi 'Cuda: the undercarriage was untouched, and no replacement parts had ever been installed; the interior had no noticeable wear, and the carpet and wooden steering wheel still looked brand-new; the paint, although it had a few parking lot scuffs, still shone like new; the chrome bumpers and other bright trim was still bright; all the glass was scratch free; and the argent paint on the shaker bubble still had the original deep luster.

"Greg admitted that he was no mechanic and never lifted the hood other than to check the oil," said Smith, who was pleased to see the carburetors still had the plastic limiter caps on the adjusting screws.

"Greg requested that all the parts [that] dealership mechanics removed from the car during tune-ups be returned. So he had the original spark plugs. The only items that were not original to the car when it came off the assembly line was the oil filter, battery, negative battery cable, and a short piece of three-eighths-inch fuel line that had begun to deteriorate."

Apparently the 'Cuda was so powerful that Peterson said he regularly consumed Rolaids to help calm his stomach. Inside the center console, Smith discovered a half-consumed package of Rolaids! Oh, and remember the small packet of tire valve extensions? Those were still in the console too.

Smith returned home but made plans to return to help Peterson get the 'Cuda running.

"On my next visit, in the spring of 2007, I told Greg I felt like I was entering King Tut's tomb," Smith said. "I wanted to get the car running but didn't want to destroy the originality, like by removing the gas tank.

"I disconnected the fuel line and pulled the distributor out to prime the oil pump. I bungee-corded a one-gallon fuel can to the firewall, and the engine fired right up. It was a beautiful thing, and it didn't even smoke."

Peterson and Smith drove the car down the street and into the driveway of the Peterson house, where the car was parked every day in the 1970s. Since that time, Peterson has asked Smith to assist him in selling the car to a collector. Smith said that at a market high several years ago, the car probably had a value of $1 million, but the current economy had brought the value down to between $600,000 and $700,000.

"We notified some of the big players in the Mopar collecting world but didn't get any real bites," Smith said. "Then we put the car on eBay and got an offer of eight hundred forty-nine thousand dollars, but the purchaser was a fraud. Today we're hoping to find someone who wants to own the best, most original Hemi on the planet.

"I can't imagine a Holier Grail."

THE REAL JOB #1 MUSTANG

The Mustang coupe sat in a driveway in Winston-Salem, North Carolina, driven hard and put away wet. After passing the car for a few months, Todd Adams knocked on the door and asked if it was for sale.

"No," the woman said. Apparently, her father had bought it new, and it had sentimental value. But a few more visits convinced her that Adams was a serious buyer.

"I had checked the serial number, number one-zero-zero-two-one-one, and knew it was a very early Mustang, definitely a Day One car," he said. "That's what purists call it." Day One means it was sold on the first day Mustang went on sale, on April 17, 1964.

Adams didn't think much of it, registered it, and drove it to his final year of high school. After he graduated in 1986, he went to college and parked the Mustang in his parents' backyard.

Adams was offered a parking space in a friend's barn in 1992, and there it sat for the next eighteen years. Adams almost forgot he even owned the car. "I went ten years without even speaking to my friend," he said.

Adams was reminded of his vintage Mustang, though, while watching the television broadcast of the 2010 Barrett-Jackson auction. "They showed a 1964 ½ Mustang Pace Car and mentioned that it was serial number one-zero-zero-two-one-two, the oldest production Mustang known to exist," he said. "I said to myself, 'I think my Mustang in the barn is older than that!'"

Hull & Dobbs is the original selling dealership in Winston-Salem, North Carolina. *Steve Mezard Jian*

He checked the title, and sure enough, it was number 100211. In fact, Adams's car was now the earliest known Job One Mustang, meaning that it is the oldest-known Mustang to have rolled off the assembly line on the first day of production, on March 9, 1964. Cars built prior to number 211 were preproduction, built as prototypes by engineers. When new, his car was loaded onto a transporter and delivered to Hull-Dobbs Ford in Winston-Salem, North Carolina, where it was sold to the father of the woman who sold it to Adams.

After the auction, Adams removed the car from the damp barn and parked it in dry, secure storage, where it has remained ever since. And Adams's Mustang is definitely a barn find—looking sad and in need of restoration, the car even has original crayon markings on the firewall and radiator support.

"The car is a real bastard," he said. "It's a mixture of production and pre-production parts. All the glass is original, and a couple of pieces were 1963 date code production. The only parts on the Mustang that are not original are the front bumper and half of the grille surround."

Adams's life has changed since buying number 100211 as a high school senior. He's a successful businessman with a family—and even another vintage Mustang. Realizing that a correct restoration would cost a small fortune, he's inclined to sell it to a collector who would appreciate such a rare car.

TOO MANY 'VETTES

We walked around with John, looking at some of the vehicles scattered around his property. Here was a 1957 Chevy two-door wagon; it was a decent car John said he bought seven or eight years ago at auction. And there were a couple of 1930s Ford pickup cabs he bought the previous day at the Carlisle flea market; he needed them to repair a third truck he is building. His collection was large and eclectic.

He said he's been in this location since 1978. And he said he has acquired too many projects.

"I want to restore six or eight cars to drive," he said. "The rest just need to go away. I just don't have the time to work on all of them. I have a deal on two cars inside, and they'll go away next week."

John specializes in rebuilding Rochester Fuel Injection units for 1950s and 1960s Corvettes. He said that alone keeps him too busy. And he builds engines. I asked about a Corvette that was sitting in the weeds.

"I worked on that car twenty years ago," he said.

"It belonged to a dentist. And the guy turned into a drug addict and never came back to get it. I don't think he's even alive anymore. It's a 1976, and it has the high-horsepower engine and a four-speed." It had been sitting there so long that much of the paint on the hood, trunk, and roof was flaking off, exposing the raw fiberglass.

We walked up to an early car, also in the weeds.

"That was the first Corvette I ever bought," he said. "It's a 1962, and I bought it without an engine. I put a built-up three twenty-seven in it, and it would pull the front wheels off the ground."

This '62 Corvette sits inside another shed. John has been into Corvettes for forty years. He's bought them for as little as $800. *Michael Alan Ross*

John has owned many of his Corvettes for decades, but this 1958 fuel-injected model was purchased just a few months before we saw it. *Michael Alan Ross*

Then there was a 1958 Corvette, which happens to be my personal favorite early-model Corvette. I really dig the faux hood vents and the two chrome strips on the trunk.

"It's a fuelie car," John said. "I bought it just like this. And there's another '58 fuelie car. I bought it about four months ago."

Man, this guy has the 'Vettes. But John is not totally a Corvette guy. There, parked next to his building, was a 1940 Ford panel truck. In what must be the oddest engine transplant of all time, the truck had a Ford 300-cubic-inch straight-six-cylinder engine—probably 1960s vintage—with a four-barrel carburetor.

"It has an Offenshauser intake manifold and a C-4 automatic transmission," he said. "And it has a Deluxe passenger car nose instead of the commercial nose. I have gathered all the parts to put this back together and bought a second truck as well."

Sounds like the typical car guy; he doesn't need the first truck, so he bought a second one. He did tell me these trucks were for sale. We were now inside his building, which was large and cluttered. John pointed out a '64 Stingray that had belonged to a friend of his.

"It got crashed about ten years ago. The owner loaned it to someone, and this guy pulled out in front of someone and the front end got knocked off. I may fix it. Time is the issue."

John said he does all his own fiberglass and paint work. He pointed out a 1932 Ford panel truck inside the cluttered building.

"It's the old Culligan truck," John said as he pointed out the lettering on the side of the body. "That's my winter project. It's going on a J&W Chassis,

One of my personal favorites in John's collection was this 1962 fuel-injected Corvette. If I owned this car, I would clean it up and use it as-is. *Michael Alan Ross*

John restores cars for customers and does all mechanical work, bodywork, and paint in his shop. This coupe is receiving major body repair. *Michael Alan Ross*

a built-up Ford three zero two with a five-speed with air conditioning. It will be a keeper and a driver."

Some of the other cars in the building: a '64 Impala SS (300 horsepower, four speed); a 1955 Chevrolet Suburban (327, automatic); a black 1966 Stingray coupe (a/c, 360 horsepower, disc brakes, original knock-off wheels, and side pipes); a 1957 Pontiac Safari wagon (rust-free Arizona car, tri-power, with a spare Smokey Yunick–built 377-cubic-inch engine); a 1965 Corvette a/c car; a 1957 Chevy sedan delivery (owned twenty-five years); a 1966 Pontiac GTO with four-speed; a 1968 Camaro RS/SS convertible; a 1962 Corvette that he uses to test run his rebuilt fuel-injection units before sending them back to customers; a 1965 Corvette coupe that John drove for a number of years; and more. John admits that he bought most of his Corvettes at the right time.

For some of them, he paid as little as eight hundred dollars. And, until recently, John also owned a Rangoon Red 289 Cobra that he purchased about forty years ago. John brought us into another garage, where he had a very nice 1940 Ford Standard sixty-horsepower coupe and the last 1966 Shelby Mustang GT350 ever built. John said he has never advertised his cars or business, and yet he has more work than he can handle.

BUYING A 427 FAIRLANE—AGAIN

Tom Von Meyer brought us to a friend's house. We pulled into the driveway, walked into the backyard, and met Joe Wiencek. And we couldn't help but notice his two 1964 Ford Fairlanes.

"I bought this Fairlane originally back in 1981 or 1982; I can't remember," Wiencek said. "There is still an inspection sticker on the windshield that was put on when I owned it. It was springtime, and I just had gotten my tax-return check, so I was heading down south to buy a car. I went with friends, and we went through Virginia and West Virginia."

Wiencek said that he actively drag raced at the time at Thompson Drag Strip near his home in Ohio. He said they'd race High School Eliminator events with cars such as 'Cudas, Road Runners, Challengers, Mustangs, and even Ford F-100s.

"I was young and free and had a pocket full of money," he said. "I'd get off at an exit that looked attractive to me and drive five or ten miles. The towns had to talk to me. If we didn't find anything, we'd get back on the highway for a while."

Wiencek saw this Fairlane on a front yard with a for-sale sign written on a shopping bag. He knocked on the door of the house.

"'Oh, that car belongs to Billy Ray,' they said. 'He's down at the corner, shooting pool.' So my buddy and I walked into the pool hall, and nobody knew who we were. I asked, 'Who is Billy Ray?' Suddenly these guys circled around me and said, 'Who wants to know?' Apparently, Billy Ray was in

Imagine connecting with your high school girlfriend thirty years later! Joe Wiencek owned this gasser Fairlane in 1981, sold it a few years later, then found it on Craigslist and bought it back. *Michael Alan Ross*

hiding. He had gotten in trouble with this car, and the police were looking for him," Wiencek said.

"I bought it for eight hundred dollars and drove it home from Waynesboro, Virginia. It had a four twenty-seven side-oiler, a four-speed, and a straight front axle. When I was driving it home, we were going through a Pittsburgh suburb and pulled into a McDonald's to get a meal. As I pulled into the parking lot, I had a little fun and chirped the rear tires a little bit."

When Wiencek and his buddy came out of McDonald's, a sheriff was leaning against the fender.

"'What do you call that little display back there?' the sheriff asked us. I told him, 'A sudden burst of energy?' The sheriff said, 'Well, that sudden burst of energy is going to cost you a hundred fifty dollars.'"

Luckily, Wiencek had his checkbook on him. He wrote a check and was back on the road in no time.

"To put these R-code engines into a Fairlane required some sledgeham-mering to make them fit," he said. He pointed out some hammer marks where the firewall met the transmission tunnel. "This car was originally a C-code car; it came with a two eighty-nine [engine] and a four-speed. I'm guessing the big-block drivetrain came out of the same Galaxie as the buckets and console came from. Maybe someone bought a wreck and transplanted all the pieces."

I'm a sucker for cars with straight front axles. I just dig the gasser look, and I have ever since I fell in love with the Stone, Woods & Cook '41 Willys coupe. Wiencek's backyard "art" was one of the coolest barn finds I've seen.

He kept the Fairlane about four or five years and had a lot of fun with it.

"Then I bought a Lincoln Continental out of Oklahoma and didn't need the Fairlane anymore," he said. "So I traded the car for a whole trunk load of guns. They were all legal—it was just an old guy who wanted to buy the car and didn't have the money, so we just traded."

And that was the last time Wiencek saw his beloved Fairlane . . . for twenty-seven years, anyway. Wiencek retired, had some health issues, and suddenly had the desire to buy another Fairlane for him and his sons to work on together.

"I wasn't getting any younger," he said. "So lo and behold, I punched in 1964 Ford Fairlane into Craigslist and maybe twelve or twenty of them came up, and my old car was one of them. I still had the photos, so I knew it was my car, although in much worse shape."

He thinks he paid too much money for it for the condition it was in and without a drivetrain—$2,800—but because it was his old car, he had to buy it back, regardless of price.

"I had a photo of me standing next to the car as a kid, and my wife took a photo of me in the exact same spot when I got it back. I asked her, 'Shelby, who looks worse today, me or the car?'"

Today the car still retains the Ford Galaxie bucket seats and console, which are in Wiencek's attic, as well as the nine-inch rear. When he owned it the first time, it rolled on Cragar S/S wheels, but he's not sure if this time around he'll install Cragars, Keystone Klassics, or Ansen aluminum slot rims. Something old school, for sure.

It seems that finding new parts for 1964 Ford Fairlanes is a challenge. Wiencek said that panels for 1966 and 1967 are reproduced but not 1964s. He is on the lookout for new rear quarter panels, as the originals have some cancer on the bottoms, and the left rear panel has a fair amount of body damage as well. (So, if anyone reading this has some perfect or NOS rear quarters for a '64 Fairlane, get in touch with me.)

Next, our attention turned to a second 1964 Fairlane parked next to his 427. "That's an honest-to-goodness K-code car," Wiencek said as he showed me the car's VIN, with the letter K in the fifth spot. "I got this car at Jim's Recycling in Attica, Michigan. Actually, he had two of them—the other was an F-code, also a sports coupe.

Wiencek was so excited about buying his old '64 Fairlane that he bought a second one! This one is an honest-to-God K-code car, which was delivered new with the 271-horsepower Hi-Po 289 engine. *Michael Alan Ross*

"So I stripped that one of the console and bucket seats before I dragged this home."

Apparently, Jim of Jim's Recycling's had an Uncle Gerald who bought the car brand new at the local dealer and raced it in Northern Michigan with the Hi-Po 289.

"In no time he blew the two eighty nine and put a four twenty-seven in it," Wiencek said. "So here I am with two former four twenty-seven Fairlanes." Today, Uncle Gerald is in a nursing home.

While we were interviewing and shooting photos, we had failed to realize that it was very hot, plus we had been driving without air conditioning. Thankfully, Shelby came out and offered us some ice water before we passed out from dehydration. Wiencek's biggest challenge now is finding an indoor workshop so he and his sons can work on the cars during the cold Michigan winter. His garage at home is occupied with daily drivers, so he is hoping to find a small industrial building to lease.

"That is stage one, because I need to keep these cars from getting any worse," he said.

Agreed.

1967 FORD COUNTRY SQUIRE

In 1966, when muscle cars were all the rage, Vincent Bowling felt left out. At a time when all his friends were buying powerful Hemi Mopars and big-block Chevys and Hi-Po Fords—and showing them off around their Dayton, Ohio, hometown—Bowling felt excluded.

"We've got three boys, and we need to take them to Little League games and school events," Bowling's wife said. "There will be no muscle cars in this family. We need a station wagon."

Of course, Bowling understood that his growing family needed a proper station wagon. Still, testosterone was flowing through his veins like Sunoco 260 fuel.

He visited his local Ford dealership, Stueve Ford, in nearby Miamisburg, Ohio. He explained his dilemma to the salesman.

"I like driving sporty cars, but I need a responsible, practical family car," he said.

In a perfect world, his dream car would be a big-block wagon that had muscle car features, such as a 428-cubic-inch engine and a four-speed gearbox.

"Well, you can order the four twenty-eight, but only with an automatic transmission," said the salesman. "And I can order you a three-speed manual on the column, but only with a two eighty-nine or three ninety engine. The codes just won't work with the four twenty-eight and four-speed."

Bowling went home, depressed but not defeated. He visited Stueve Ford several more times and continued to press the issue.

Finally, the salesman, clearly frustrated, offered Bowling a name and address at Ford Motor Company. "Write a letter to this guy at Ford," he said. "If he gives his okay, we'll build it."

That night, Bowling fired off a letter listing the specs for the car he'd like to order and the reason he needed such an unusual car.

A few weeks later, a letter arrived from the gentleman at Ford, saying they would build his dream car.

The name of that Ford employee? Lee Iacocca, at the time vice president of Ford's Car and Truck Group.

Victory!

Bowling brought the letter to the salesman, and the two sat down and wrote an order.

One rare beast! I discovered this 1967 Ford Country Squire in a Detroit suburb in 2016. Besides having an attractive layer of patina, the wagon is equipped with some race performance options. *John Davison*

The base car would be a Country Squire four-door wagon in Sauterne Gold. It was ordered with most of the luxury accessories available at the time: white wall tires, a luggage rack, courtesy lights, tinted glass, deluxe seat belts, an AM/FM radio, power steering and windows, and Selectaire Conditioning. Then, on a special-order form, the performance items were added: the base 289-cubic-inch engine—a $106.72 option over the standard six-cylinder—was upgraded to a 428, four-barrel Thunderbird engine for an upcharge of $244.77. A four-speed transmission was added at the additional cost of $184.02. XL-type bucket seats ($81.90) and an XL console ($48.81) were added.

Check this out: a four-speed manual gearbox, bucket seats, and a console. This would be a rare option package for a coupe, sedan or convertible, but a wagon? *John Davison*

Bowling wanted dual exhaust but was told that because station wagons had a gas tank in the left-side rear quarter panel, dual exhaust would not be possible because the fuel would get too hot. That wasn't a deal breaker, so he continued with the order. Oddly, even though front disc brakes were available as an option on the big Ford, Bowling decided to stick with the standard drum brakes.

Bowling signed the purchase order, and the salesman sent the one-of-a-kind order off to Dearborn. He had his concerns that at the end of the day, the car might not actually be approved for production by Ford management, but he kept his fingers crossed.

A couple of months later, the salesman called. "Your car has arrived!"

The impossible dream had come true; the "we-can't-build-it" Ford station wagon would soon be sitting in his garage.

The car, which was built at Ford's Louisville, Kentucky, plant, had a base price of $3,359.06. By the time Bowling finished adding about $1,500 worth of upgrades and options, plus transportation charges, the car cost $4,915.33. Even when calculating for inflation, in 2017, it would still be a bargain at about $36,000.

The Bowling family enjoyed their unique Country Squire for ten years, during which time it likely transported kids to numerous baseball games, hauled home tons of groceries, and carried many Christmas trees on the roof rack. And hopefully Vincent flexed his wagon's powerful drivetrain when he socialized with his muscle car–driving friends.

In 1977, the Bowling family sold the one-of-one wagon to Jim Lewis of Yellow Springs, Ohio. Lewis was a car guy and displayed the unusual wagon at car shows and Ford meets for a number of years. But eventually he parked the car in his driveway, where it sat for a long time.

Ford Galaxy collector Adrian Clements from Michigan heard rumors of the wagon through a network of friends. He visited Lewis, saw the car in a rather neglected state, and offered to buy it. On September 9, 2001—two days before the 9/11 attacks—Clements trailered home the non-running car.

"The exterior was covered in mildew after sitting outside in Ohio for years and years," Clements said. "The body had some rot—the bottom of the quarters, doors, and tailgate—but the interior was dry."

Within two days, Clements had the car running, and then he began scrubbing the mildew from the body. He rebuilt the engine, fuel system, brakes, and cooling system.

The station wagon became a star wherever Clements drove it: the All-Ford Nationals in Carlisle and the Ford Centennial celebration at the manufacturer's headquarters in 2003.

In 2016, I was in the Detroit area researching a project later published as *Motor City Barn Finds*. Before I departed my home in North Carolina for Detroit, I posted a notice on Facebook that I would be searching for neglected and forgotten cars in the Detroit area, and if anyone had suggestions, I was all ears. My friend Zach Straits, whose barn-find Camaro appeared in my book *50 Shades of Rust*, sent me contact information for Clements.

When I arrived in Detroit, I gave Clements a call. He told me the story of his unique car and invited me to take a look.

I arrived at the mini-storage facility, saw the wagon, and instantly fell in love.

I was working with photographer Michael Alan Ross, who snapped photos while I carefully inspected the car. I was smitten.

Michael and I continued our journey, searching for more cars, but I couldn't get the wagon out of my head, especially when Clements told me that he was relocating to New York City and would be selling the Country Squire.

Two months passed, and I called him again so he could fill in some details on the story I was writing. He still had the car, but he needed to sell it soon.

I spoke to my wife, Pat, and told her this station wagon "spoke to me." I clearly didn't need another car—I owned too many already—but this car was different.

"If it's as special as you say, you should buy it," she said.

Bingo!

I called Clements, made him an offer, he counter-offered, and I accepted. The one-of-a-kind wagon would be mine.

I have a soft spot in my heart for station wagons. I still own the 1939 Ford Woody that I bought as a fifteen-year-old in 1969 and the 1953 Ford two-door Ranch Wagon I bought as a high school senior. This wagon would round out my collection nicely.

It seems that I'm not the only person who appreciates station wagons. Wagons, along with pickup trucks, were often driven hard and put away wet, so finding examples in good condition these days is rare. Making this car even more rare are the unusual performance accessories.

I started driving the wagon and quickly realized it needed some mechanical work to make it totally roadworthy. For one, the original Autolite 4300 four-barrel carburetor was known to be troublesome even when new, but this one was especially so. It apparently dumped excess fuel into the exhaust system, where it collected in the muffler. Occasionally, a huge backfire would have bystanders ducking for cover and looking for bomb craters.

I reviewed the options—buy a new carb, rebuild the original, etc.—and made an unusual decision. I installed a fuel injection unit, which I truly love. It fits under the original air cleaner and cannot be detected when the hood is open. Plus, the car starts easily in cold weather and gets better gas mileage.

Second, I installed disc brakes up front. Having driven this car around town with the original drum brakes, I felt an upgrade was necessary.

Now, don't get all excited that I am hot rodding this wagon: I saved the original carburetor and drum brakes, and if I ever restore the car, I will reinstall them.

Oh, and I plan to repair the cancer on the lower body panels so that the car doesn't deteriorate further.

Since taking ownership of the car, I have driven it from North Carolina to McPherson College in Kansas. It drove as smoothly as a Lincoln, and with a rear-end ratio of 2:73, I had to watch out for radar traps because it liked to creep up to one hundred miles per hour.

I have also used the car for a couple of episodes of my *Barn Find Hunter* YouTube series, which is produced by Hagerty Insurance. The car never fails to grab attention wherever I drive it.

I am so fortunate to be this Country Squire's current caretaker, and I look forward to many more miles and many more years of ownership.

AN ARIZONA BARN FIND: BRONCO RACER

BY TODD ZUERCHER

Like so many vehicles today that are vaunted as barn finds, this truck wasn't actually resting in a barn when we found it, because there just aren't a lot of barns in Arizona. However, like much of home equity–financed America, Arizona does have a lot of trailers. And this particular Bronco was sitting in one of those trailers for six or seven years before it was rescued.

In the early 1990s, I joined the Arizona Classic Bronco Club and soon met a fellow club member who was rebuilding an old Bill Stroppe Racing Bronco into a sand toy to run in the dunes at several locations in the southwestern United States. The club member had found the Bronco in pieces in Boulder City, Nevada, several years earlier but didn't know any of its prior history.

Having an interest in both off-road racing and Bronco history, I immediately realized the significance and rarity of such a vehicle, but I wasn't interested in purchasing it. I saw the Bronco a number of times in the following years at various club events and even ventured to the Glamis Sand Dunes with the owner in the late 1990s and saw it in action.

Thanks to the Internet, I met another Bronco brother-in-arms: Andrew Norton of Petaluma, California. Andrew was already the nation's leading expert on the 1971–1975 Bill Stroppe–built Baja Broncos, so expanding his knowledge to include the racing Broncos was a natural one. Andrew and I grew to be friends through our mutual love of the Stroppe vehicles. The race truck in Arizona became our little secret; we didn't want someone else finding it and trying to buy it.

Bronco Buddies Todd Zuercher and Andrew Norton restored this former desert racer to its condition when it was constructed by Bill Stroppe in the 1970s. *Dave Loewen*

As the century drew to a close, the Stroppe owner was less involved in club activities and eventually left the club. Thankfully, we kept in contact. After a few years, the Bronco's owner stopped going to the dunes. The Bronco was parked in an enclosed trailer on the owner's property in Phoenix.

With interest in vintage Stroppe vehicles growing, Andrew and I agreed that if it ever became available at the right price, we would buy it together.

I continued to keep in contact with the owner—stopping in at his work to say hello and corresponding once or twice a year via email. I decided to stay in contact. Chatting about it occasionally might keep us on the radar if the owner decided to sell the Bronco.

In March 2008, I checked my email one evening and saw a message from the owner with "Bronco" in the subject line. I didn't even have to open it to know what it was about. I was pleasantly surprised the owner's asking price was within $1,000 of what Andrew and I wanted to pay. I called Andrew immediately and we decided that night to buy it, even though we didn't really know the Bronco's true history.

With the deal completed, the Bronco was delivered to my home several weeks later; its uncorked Hi-Po 289 V-8 rattled the walls as it emerged from its resting place in the trailer for the first time in many years.

The Bronco ran, though not well, and its transmission barely had enough hydraulic force to move the truck around. The interior was packed with sand from its many trips to the dunes, and the front axle was bent on the passenger's side—a casualty from many years of racing and perhaps some airborne antics in the sand dunes.

Thankfully, the truck came with several boxes of original parts and pieces, which Andrew and I counted as a blessing, considering the number of owners it had since leaving Stroppe's shop in the 1970s.

Then our research started. What did we really have? We found a VIN on the vehicle's data plate, indicating it was the first production vehicle for 1968.

Our next step was to contact renowned Ford expert Kevin Marti at Marti Auto Works in Peoria, Arizona, who has all the Ford production records from 1967 to 2012. Marti didn't have records for any vehicle configured like this Bronco in 1968, so his best guess was that it was a prototype or engineering mule—exactly the type of Bronco that Ford would've given to Bill Stroppe to build into a race truck.

Being a bit of a historical packrat, I had collected nearly every off-road magazine published in the 1960s and 1970s and stored them in a backyard shed. Several months after the Bronco's purchase, Andrew and I spent a weekend going through all those old magazines, making copies of any and all Stroppe racing Bronco photos we could find.

Some additional clues emerged when we examined the truck more closely and crawled underneath it. Luckily, key pieces of the suspension, frame, and body helped provide more information about the truck's identity.

As Andrew and I pored over the photos, magazines, and videos and compared the features of our Bronco to the documentation, the pedigree of our truck became clear to us. We not only had a Stroppe racing Bronco, but a very special one indeed.

In 1969, off-road racers Larry Minor and Rod Hall, both of Hemet, California, drove a freshly built racing Bronco to the overall victory in the 1969 NORRA Mexican 1000 (now known as the Baja 1000) with a time of twenty hours and thirty-eight minutes. They not only beat all the other four-wheeled vehicles, but all the motorcycles as well. It was the first time that a four-wheeled vehicle won overall and the only time that a four-wheel-drive vehicle finished first overall.

Based on the photos and information we collected, we knew we had the '69 1000 winner in our hands.

After its 1969 win, the Bronco compiled an impressive racing resume over the course of six seasons, collecting five first-place wins and four second-place finishes with Rod Hall and several other drivers behind the wheel.

Like so many race cars, the truck was finished in a variety of liveries over several seasons. Acting like a dendrochronologist who can analyze the life of a tree by looking at its rings, Andrew analyzed the truck's history by slowly removing the various layers of paint at several points along the Bronco's body. His analysis showed the colors matched the various years' paint schemes found in vintage color photos and magazines.

As is sometimes the case with vintage racing vehicles, there was some contention on whether the truck really was the 1969 winner. Through careful analysis of the period photos and videos available, and matching numerous key physical characteristics on the '69 winner not found on any other truck other than ours, Andrew and I are steadfast in our belief that the evidence is in our favor.

A period racing photo, likely from 1975, based on the front fender points-championship decal. Zuercher and Norton figure they own the 1969 NORRA Mexican 1000 winner! *David Kier*

Memories fade over time, particularly with regard to small details, as we found when trying to piece together the Bronco's history. As former Stroppe team racer Carl Jackson remarked a few years ago, "If I had known you were going to be asking all these questions so many years later, I would have paid more attention!"

In concert with the collection of documentation, Andrew and I slowly worked on the truck as time allowed, removing its dune-running livery and getting it back to drivable condition. We made small changes here and there until the fall of 2009, when another email arrived.

That email was from Chris Wilson—a friend, longtime off-road racer, and Baja 1000 winner. He was inquiring whether I knew of any historically significant Broncos that might be available for Chris and his codriver to drive in the newly reborn NORRA Mexican 1000 race. I mentioned several possibilities, with our Stroppe Bronco being the most obvious choice. After some discussion with Andrew and an analysis of the risks involved, a deal was reached whereby Chris and Glen Straightiff, his codriver, would rebuild and restore the Bronco as historically correct as possible in exchange for driving the vehicle in the event. We knew this was a great way to get a lot of the mechanical work done on the truck.

Four months later, the freshly painted and mechanically rebuilt Bronco was completed just in time for the race. Once again, it looked like a real race truck.

Chris and Glen started the race on the morning of April 28, 2010, in Mexicali, Baja California, and finished three days later in La Paz, covering more than 1,100 miles in the process. Spurning the electronic navigation and communication aids of many of their competitors, they raced as the Stroppe team did in the sixties and seventies, without GPS or radios and wearing open-face helmets.

Despite getting lost twice, they managed to finish first in their class. The little Bronco obviously had not lost its knack for winning races after a thirty-five-year absence from Baja.

In the intervening years, Andrew and I raced the Bronco in the 2012 NORRA Mexican 1000 and displayed it at the prestigious Art Center College of Design annual car show in Pasadena, California. And, thanks to Andrew's connections, it had a bit part in the movie *Need for Speed*. After the movie appearance, it received a fresh coat of period-correct paint and new graphics and now occasionally appears at car shows and cruises the Oregon sand dunes. Andrew and I enjoy sharing our treasure with other enthusiasts and sharing its vast history and the story of how it made a full circle back to its former glory.

DUAL SOLDIER COUGAR

For all the horror brought on by the Vietnam War, the conflict had at least one somewhat positive aspect: it was good for the automobile industry.

Before shipping out, when home on leave, or after discharge from the service, soldiers often paid a visit to the local car dealership to purchase the latest models. During the time they performed their military service in either the US Army, Navy, Air Force, or Marines, these young people missed out on much of our changing culture. So when they came home, they were eager to catch up on music, the sexual revolution, and, alas, muscle cars.

And those car dealerships were ready and waiting for them. No matter what brand of car a soldier might be loyal to, there was a high-performance model guaranteed to leave twin black stripes on the pavement upon exiting the dealership.

This story is about one of those purchases.

First off, all the players in this story have the same last name: Powell. Paul Powell had just left college and enlisted in the service. But before shipping out to Vietnam, he was yearning to reward himself with a hot set of wheels. He asked his older brother, William "Tex" Powell, to help him shop for a car.

Being a Ford guy, Paul first visited Jack Roach Ford near his home in Houston. He was instantly smitten with the Shelby GT500 sitting in the showroom. But he couldn't afford the car payments or the insurance, so he kept shopping.

His next stop: Dave Snelling Lincoln-Mercury, also in Houston. A Mercury Cougar GTE—a rare model featuring a 427 side-oiler racing engine—was sitting on the showroom floor, but again, the purchase price and insurance cost took that car out of consideration.

Paul finally settled on an XR7 model. It was nicely accessorized, powered by a 390-cubic-inch engine featuring 320 horsepower and 427 lb-ft of torque. It had a C-6 automatic, power steering and brakes, air conditioning, and leather seats. It was badged as a 6.5 liter and had the optional heavy-duty suspension. The car had enough power to satisfy his desires and was still affordable.

Older brother Tex, seven years Paul's senior, helped him purchase the car by putting the title in his name, thereby reducing the insurance rates.

Standing quietly in the background and observing his first dealership transaction was eight-year-old Bill, Tex's oldest son. Paul, still in the military, drove his Cougar with gusto for a number of years, but with the gas crisis of the early 1970s and the needs of his growing family, he parked it with about ninety thousand miles on the odometer. The Cougar was put into storage.

That's the end of Part One of this story.

Bill Powell's 1967 390 Cougar is protected from the elements, but the open-sided barn still allowed the car to be used for pigeon target practice. *Bill Powell*

Part Two begins when Bill Powell (remember eight-year-old Bill watching his father and uncle buy the Cougar?) assumed ownership of the "family" Cougar.

Bill was now a young man, and in 1978, the Cougar became his first set of wheels. He admits that he was an immature young guy and that preservation of a future classic car was not on his mind.

"The torque and horsepower was always there, and it was easy to overwhelm those fourteen-inch wheels and stock brakes," he said.

Six years later, Bill joined the army and shipped out to Oahu, Hawaii. Later that year, Tex (remember, he's the dad) trailered the Cougar to Charleston, South Carolina, and shipped it to his son in Hawaii.

Four years later, in 1988, the Cougar was shipped back to Charleston when Bill transferred from Hawaii to North Carolina.

"My younger brother, Mike, parked the car in an outbuilding on a friend's farm in North Carolina," Bill said. "I decided to keep it parked there until I had the time and resources to restore it properly. I was resuming my college education and working toward an Army officer's commission."

Bill didn't park the car because he didn't enjoy driving it though. "At the time, there were very few Cougar-specific parts being reproduced," he said. "I believed if I continued driving the car I would wear it out and damage it beyond realistic repair."

So the Cougar was parked in 1988 with the best of intentions.

"I always believed restoration of my car was just around the corner, but that was never reality," Bill said. "The car is still sitting exactly where I parked it in 1988 with surprisingly little damage. Sure, the rodents have done some damage to the interior insulation, but nothing else beyond a spectacular coat of dust and cobwebs."

Bill attributes the car's surprisingly sound condition to the fact that it is parked in the center of the outbuilding, far enough from the building's edges that rain and snow never reach it.

Many of the women in Bill's life have driven the Cougar. His aunt Kathy drove the car while his uncle Paul was serving in Vietnam. His mother drove it, and his brother Mike's wife, Sharon, drove it when she was a teenager.

"There is no shortage of stories regarding this car," he said. "It's really part of our family's history."

Bill, who today lives in Ohio and has retired from the military, said he tries to visit the car when he visits his family in North Carolina. But thirty years later, the Cougar is still obediently sitting there, waiting for that promised attention.

TWO STUFFED PONCHOS

Leads are worth following up on, even if they sound too good to be true. Granted, 99 percent of the time if you hear about a Chevy in a barn, it will be a rusty Citation. But maybe, just maybe, it could turn out to be a Corvette.

Scott Happel has been a General Motors fan since he was a kid, and his father was the service manager at the local Pontiac/Buick dealership in Allentown, Pennsylvania.

"My buddy told me there was a woman who wanted two old Chevys hauled out of her garage and brought to the junkyard," said Happel, sixty-four, who still lives in Allentown. "I had a rollback [truck], so I went to the woman's house to see what she had.

"She said she didn't own the two cars but that she rented the garage to a man who was years behind in his rent. She wanted the garage empty so she could rent it out to someone else."

Scott peaked into the garage and saw two covered cars, but he couldn't tell what they were. He squeezed inside the tight quarters.

"They weren't Chevys, but Pontiacs," he said. "The two were jammed into a one-and-a-half car garage. It was so tight that I couldn't walk between the cars."

When he started to lift up the covers on the cars, he wanted to scream at his good fortune. But he couldn't because the woman was standing beside him and he didn't want her to know how valuable the cars were.

One car, the one on the left, was a 1965 Pontiac Grand Prix. It had fifty-four thousand miles on the odometer, a 389 engine, a 400 automatic, and twenty-seven factory options.

The car on the right he couldn't have imagined in his wildest dreams. It was a 1965 Pontiac Catalina 2+2. In the dark garage, Scott ran his hands across the side of the fenders. He felt a 421 logo, meaning it had Pontiac's largest motor. He lifted the hood and couldn't tell if it had a single four-barrel carburetor, but as he started to run his hand over the side of the carburetors, he could feel three distinct units under the air cleaner.

When he was able to shimmy down the side and look into the side window of the Catalina, he discovered the car was equipped with a factory four-speed, bucket seats, and a console. *Scott Happel*

It had tri-power.

Scott shimmied down the side and saw a four-speed shifter.

This was a happy day.

But before he could remove the cars, he had to go through six months' worth of working with lawyers so he could claim legal ownership of them.

"It took one thousand hours before I could own the cars," he said. It was consuming his life.

"My wife was worried that I would lose my health over these cars."

When he paid all the legal fees and the past-due garage rental fees, he finally was able to remove the cars from the woman's garage where they had been entombed for twenty-seven years.

"I went to Harbor Freight and bought roller dollies because it was so tight in the garage," he said. "The concrete cracked on the garage floor as we wheeled the cars out. I was afraid the woman was going to make me pay for a new floor."

Scott's older brother, Robert, helped him remove the cars, so Scott let him have the Grand Prix. Robert installed new rubber door seals, underhood insulation, and an exhaust system in the Grand Prix.

Robert kept the car until recently, but sold it, his 2012 Corvette, and his pickup truck.

"Robert had massive heart attack, so he bought a new 2017 Corvette and wants to do a lot of living while he can," Scott explained.

It was the white Catalina that Scott really wanted.

"I was like a kid in a candy store," he said. "The car had only fifteen thousand seven hundred fifty-two miles on the odometer. When I uncovered it, it was like a brand-new car, only dusty."

Scott has enjoyed the car since buying it a couple of years ago. With it, he won the prestigious Historic Preservation of Original Features (HPOF) award, presented each October by the Antique Automobile Club of America (AACA) at the Hershey National Meet. His car has also been written up in numerous Pontiac magazine stories.

Through a stroke of good luck, Scott found out the Catalina's first owner was a woman in Maryland, Evelyn Barnhardt, and it was drag raced.

"I don't think Evelyn drag raced it herself, but probably her kids raced it," he explained. "The car has virtually no options. It was ordered with the big motor, tri-power, a four-speed, eight-lug wheels, and a 4:11 posi rear, but it does not have power steering, power brakes, or air conditioning. It's just a stripper car with an AM radio and four-wheel drum brakes."

Recently, Scott acquired a drag racing home video that features his Pontiac. It was filmed in the late sixties at Mason Dixon Dragway in Maryland.

Lately, Scott has been considering selling the car. He said he feels nervous about leaving the car unattended in parking lots, but it's mostly because he and his wife have experienced health issues. He'd like to sell the car to a collector and buy something that is less valuable and easier to enjoy.

Maybe he'll be lucky enough to find another car in an old garage.

"This car was asleep for twenty-seven years," he said. "They're still out there—they're just asleep."

STUMBLING UPON AN SCCA CHAMPION

Steve Silverstein is a Sunbeam collector. Unlike most Sunbeam collectors who seek out only the very desirable Ford V-8-powered Tigers, Silverstein truly appreciates the Tiger's less-powerful sibling, the Alpine. Alpine Series IVs were powered by 1,600cc four-cylinder engines that produced eighty-seven horsepower, and they were capable sports cars in their day. So capable, in fact, that the manufacturer, Rootes Group, decided to field some factory-backed entries in amateur sports car races during the 1960s against some very formidable competition from both MG and Triumph. As it turned out, the entries were surprisingly successful.

Scanning the Sunbeam Alpine Owner's Club website in early 2000, Silverstein zeroed in on a particular ad: "Alpine Race Car For Sale—Freshly Machined Engine." The machined engine caught his attention because the oil pressure in his own street Alpine's engine was on the decline. When he arrived at the owner's home, he saw that the car was in worse condition than he was led to believe. He suspected that the engine block was cracked, and very little of the car's history was known. But there were a number of new old stock (NOS) parts included in the deal, and most of the chrome and trim pieces were in good condition, so he struck a deal for what was to be an Alpine parts car.

When the newly acquired Alpine Series IV arrived at Silverstein's Marlboro, Massachusetts, home, his wife, Ellen, wasn't too impressed. They began to unload boxes of spare parts onto shelves in the basement when Ellen discovered at least a hundred receipts. She caught her husband's attention when she

Don Sessler (in helmet) drove this Sunbeam to the 1964 SCCA F-Production National Championship. Here he takes one of many victory laps with his wife and crew. *Steve Silverstein*

began to read some of the notes out loud: "New Koni shocks for Daytona, '67." She also found some postcards from one of the car's former owners, Dan Carmichael. An Internet search revealed that Carmichael was an accomplished road racer who raced Sunbeams for the Sports Car Forum in Columbus, Ohio.

Silverstein's interest was piqued, and he ran to his bookshelves to discover that the Sunbeam he had just purchased may have been more than simply a club racer back in the 1960s. In the book *Tiger, Alpine, Rapier* by Richard Langworth, Silverstein came across the name Don Sessler, who won the SCCA F-Production National Championship in 1964. He called Sessler and confirmed that the car he had just purchased was not your everyday racing Alpine, but the actual championship car that both he and Carmichael had raced as half of a two-car, Alpine/Tiger team. Suddenly, Ellen felt better about the purchase.

As discovered, the Alpine's body was sound, probably due to the fact that it had been stored indoors from 1968 to 1998. The only previous damage had been on the car's right front fender, which had been hit by another Alpine when Carmichael was competing in the 1965 American Road Race of Champions. Silverstein decided to refurbish the old race car rather than restore it, so instead of a new paint job, he used compound to bring luster back to the car's forty-year-old paint finish. The interior hasn't been changed: Armor-All was used on the original seats and tonneau cover, and a thorough washing of the interior and floorpans cleansed thirty years of grime and achieved a certain patina that restored cars can never match.

The engine was a bit more of a challenge. Oilzum lubricant had gummed up the internals, requiring a thorough soaking to free up the pistons. In the process, Silverstein found that the engine block had been changed at some point from a standard 1,600cc engine to a replacement 1,725cc block. Interestingly, the cylinder head had once been modified by Joe Mondello, a renowned West Coast tuner usually associated with Oldsmobile V-8 drag racing engines.

Sunbeam Alpine No. 74 is now back on the track, as Silverstein often races the car in eastern vintage sports car events. I featured Silverstein in a March 2004 *Road & Track* magazine story about the Lime Rock Vintage Fall Festival. At Lime Rock, Silverstein is roughly 1.5 seconds slower than when original racer Sessler lapped the track at 1 minute, 13 seconds. But he told me he was having the best time of his life and hoped that his lap times would get faster. Both car and driver epitomize what vintage racing is all about: racing famous and not-so-famous sports cars, but mostly having fun.

Since his acquisition in 2000, Silverstein has accumulated a huge amount of documentation on his once semi-famous car, including race results, practice times, and preparation notes. The Sunbeam won both the 1964 National F-Production Championship with Sessler as driver and the 1964 Divisional Championship with Carmichael driving. In the process, the car chalked up an impressive number of first- and second-place finishes by both Sessler (1964) and Carmichael (1964 to 1967).

Silverstein has also corresponded with both drivers, who are in their seventies. In fact, Sessler attended the Alpine Owners Club convention in 2001, where he was thrilled to once again be reunited with his car.

THE MISSING LIGHTWEIGHT

Hidden deep inside a California garage sat a long-buried time capsule. This treasure, a rare aluminum Jaguar E-Type, had been there for more than three decades and was still undiscovered, even though scores of Jaguar collectors from around the world had been searching for the "missing lightweight." Yes, the racer eluded even the most diligent car hunters. And it's pretty safe to assume that if its eccentric owner, Howard Gidovlenko, hadn't died, the famous race car would still be hidden.

Four decades before Gidovlenko's car was unearthed, the first two Lightweight E-Types, number S850660 and number S850659, were rushed through production in order to compete in the Sebring twelve-hour race in March 1963. The former car is now recognized as the first production lightweight. It was sold to Briggs Cunningham and entered at Sebring for drivers Bruce McLaren and Walt Hansgen. The second Jag (and the subject of this story) was sold to the company's West Coast importer, Kjell Qvale, for $5,000 on October 29, 1963.

The cars were eventually flown from England to Miami and transported to the track. There was a problem, though: both cars carried the Cunningham racing colors of white with blue stripes. Thanks to some quick thinking and a can of red paint found in a Sebring hanger, Qvale's car soon looked different from the other Jag.

The cars were visually identical to their E-Type street brethren. Except for the drivetrain, which consisted of a 315-horsepower dry sump, injected 3.8-liter aluminum engine, and five-speed ZF gearbox, they were very close to stock.

This rare and missing Jaguar Lightweight E-Type was discovered in a San Francisco garage. The car had only competed in two races—the 1963 Sebring twelve-hour event and a, SCCA race at Laguna Seca before it was parked with only 2,663 miles on it. *John Mayston-Taylor*

Qvale's car was driven by Ed Leslie and Frank Morrill to a seventh-place overall finish with 195 laps completed—14 laps fewer than the winning Ferrari 250P but first in class and one position higher than Cunningham's car. Leslie's and Morrill's Sebring performance proved to be the best of any of the lightweights in a top-level long-distance event.

At the conclusion of the Sebring race, Leslie drove the car—complete with racing livery, open exhaust, and a suitcase strapped to the trunk—back to Miami, where it was air freighted to San Francisco for its next race in June. The race was held at Laguna Seca and was the third round of SCCA's United States Road Racing Championship series. This time Leslie drove the car solo, where he finished eighth. (Chuck Parsons won the race in a Lotus 23.)

After the Laguna Seca race, Qvale had the Jag transported to his dealership in San Francisco. It remained there until October, when it was purchased by World War II decorated RAF flying ace Gidovlenko. He bought the car for $5,000 at the financed rate of $143.83 per month. His intention was to begin campaigning the Jag at the 1964 24 Hours of Daytona, and he began preparing for the season by purchasing numerous spare parts from the factory. Included in the parts were three new sets of Dunlop lightweight wheels, a set of new tires, camshaft blanks, brake sets, and spare clutches.

Gidovlenko also began modifying the car based on his knowledge of aircraft technology. He used boxed sections of aluminum to brace and strengthen the

Jag's shell, and he treated the car's exposed aluminum interior panels with zinc chromate, an etching primer. Then, after dropping the rear suspension, removing the engine, and covering the body with a film of oil, he put the car into an owner-induced coma for the next thirty-five years. In fact, there's no record of Gidovlenko ever driving the car. When it was discovered on February 28, 1998, the 1963 license tags were unused.

When Gidovlenko died, his family was clearing out his personal effects at his house in early 1988, and family members eventually made it to the two garages. "In the second garage—the one at the end of the garden—they began to go through the pile of empty cardboard boxes that actually covered the Jag," said John Mayston-Taylor, chairman of Lynx Motors, who ultimately purchased the car for a private collector. "At first, they believed it was simply an old E-Type, but when they posted details of the car on the Internet, they were besieged by dealers, brokers, and opportunists from around the world who tried to convince Gidovlenko's heirs they would take if off their hands for a fraction of its value."

Gidovlenko's executor, Denis Darger, a retired Los Angeles narcotics police-man, decided it would be best to consult Jaguar expert Terry Larson. His family agreed that since the car was the major part of Gidovlenko's estate, it should be auctioned off to get the best price for it. RM Auction in Monterey, California, was given the task of hosting the event.

Interest in the car, of course, was very high, especially because the Jag only had a mere 2,663 miles on its odometer, meaning that the car had traveled farther by airplane—first from England to Florida, then to San Francisco—than it ever traveled on its wheels!

The car also had a great history. Jaguar had committed to build a dedicated competition version of its new E-Type after it competed successfully against the likes of the Ferrari 250 GTO in 1961. The factory first made a light, steel-bodied version, but no records have been found to show that the car was actually raced. The factory then built eleven aluminum-bodied lightweight roadsters for the 1963 season to compete in the GT World Championship. By that time, Enzo Ferrari realized the E-Type's promise and constructed the "Jag Beater"—the all-conquering GTO—in response.

Rather than campaigning the cars itself, Jaguar sold the lightweights to privateers who entered them in races across Europe, Australia, Africa, and the United States—where they faced stiff competition from Ferraris and Cobras. Before Gidovlenko's family uncovered number S850660, all of the other light-weights had been accounted for, leaving this car as the mystery enthusiasts dubbed "the missing lightweight."

While the car had been virtually untouched for years, it did have rough patches of bare aluminum on its body, which didn't seem to fit with the meticulous manner in which Gidovlenko had stored his prized Jag. Later on, family members concluded that the patches were apparently created during a divorce settlement, when the owner purposely roughed up the car in order to reduce its perceived value.

Fast forward thirty-plus years: the Jaguar indeed proved to be a good investment, rough patches and all. Mayston-Taylor bought it with an $872,050 bid on behalf of an anonymous client. Not a bad bit of appreciation, considering the car's original bill states that Qvale purchased the car as a demonstrator on October 29, 1963, for $5,000.

The plan was for the car to be spirited off to the Lynx shops in Hastings, England, for analysis and resurrection, but US authorities made things more difficult by refusing to believe that an E-Type could be worth so much money. They suspected a money laundering scheme. Eventually, the car was finally released and loaded onto a 747 cargo jet (transported by air yet again!) to be shipped to Lynx.

The new owner planned to preserve the car's originality, but after a thorough inspection at Lynx, he decided to refurbish rather than restore. The car would not be repainted; instead, Lynx would carefully blend new paint with the original paint to refinish the hood, doors, and rear bodywork that had been scuffed to the bare aluminum during Gidovlenko's divorce. The original paint had faded to three different tints, so a custom blend of the three colors was "soft-masked" and blown in.

The Jag's suspension was dismantled and crack-checked, which surprisingly revealed stress fractures from just the two races. The car's structure was further reinforced in the area of the roll bar, where strengthening plates were inserted. Additionally, a modern fuel cell was inserted inside the original gas tank.

Nearly all the original engine parts were reused, including the connecting rods, piston rings, cams, and valves. Only the head studs, the water pump impeller, and bearings were renewed.

Additionally, two gauges were added. One gauge would record fuel pressure (below 100 psi could burn a piston), and the other gauge would be for engine oil temperature.

The Jag's rejuvenation took only three months—incredible, considering that it was disassembled down to the smallest detail. When completed, the car was shaken down at Goodwood in the capable hands of professional

Back on the track after so many years. The Lightweight E-Type shows off its recent refurbishment by Lynx Motors. It eventually entered in the Sebring historic races and the Monterey historics at the two tracks it had competed on forty years earlier. *John Mayston-Taylor*

road racer Andy Wallace. Wallace had won the 24 Hours of Le Mans driving a Jaguar XJR in 1988.

The car's new owner wanted it to compete on the same circuits it had in 1963, so in March 1999, it was entered in the Sebring vintage races wearing the same No. 23 that it had worn there thirty-six years prior. Even though this car was "vintage" in every sense of the word compared to more modernized vintage cars, driver Mayston-Taylor finished remarkably well: third overall and first in class. In September 1999, the car was shipped to San Francisco, where it competed in the Monterey historic races, its second race at that circuit in thirty-six years. One interested spectator was the car's original driver, Ed Leslie, who has since passed away but was then a resident of nearby Carmel. Leslie rode as a passenger in parade laps as an emotional Mayston-Taylor loped around the Laguna Seca circuit with the man who piloted this very car during another time.

During the race, Mayston-Taylor was again impressive, finishing twelfth overall behind the V-8 muscle of Shelbys, Cobras, and Corvettes. So ends an amazing story about an amazing car that literally came full circle.

A CRUSADE TO BROOKLYN

Curt Vogt was scared. He felt vulnerable as he sat up in the cab of the flatbed truck on a street in the worst neighborhood in Brooklyn, New York. After all, he was unarmed and had just given $10,000 in cash to a stranger.

He prayed the reward was worth the risk.

For a couple of years, Vogt had been following leads in pursuit of one of the most sought-after Mustang drag cars of the 1960s. "I've always been a Ford guy," said Vogt, the owner of Cobra Automotive, a Shelby restoration business in Wallingford, Connecticut. "Even when I was a kid, I knew when I bought my first car, it was going to be a Mustang."

And so it was. Vogt turned seventeen in 1976 and bought a 1968 Shelby GT500KR convertible for $1,900 using money he earned mowing lawns, washing dishes, and doing other odd jobs. He sold the convertible in 1980, but the car left a mark on the young enthusiast. Since then, Vogt has owned somewhere between seventy-six and seventy-eight Shelby Mustangs—so many he isn't sure of the precise number.

Under his photo in the 1977 Amity High School yearbook, this line was printed: "Baseball, hot dogs, apple pie and Ford—Death to Chevys!"

Vogt began buying and selling Ford high-performance cars after high school. He purchased his first Fairlane Thunderbolt for $350, a car that now sells for several hundred times that amount. He owned a lot of lightweight Galaxies, one purchased for just $450. But one car always represented the Holy Grail to Vogt. This was a car he would go to any lengths to own, including handing over ten grand to a total stranger in a bad neighborhood in the middle of Brooklyn. Vogt's Holy Grail was an A/FX Mustang drag car. He had tracked down and restored one. The prospect of a second was as irresistible as it was improbable.

One of the rare Holman-Moody-built A/FX Mustangs, pictured here in 1967 or 1968 when the car was driven by Jerry Harvey and Hubert Platt. The car, one of eleven built, was based on a stock Mustang fastback with unibody construction. *Curt Vogt collection*

This is an extremely rare factory-built race car, one of only eleven constructed in 1965. One was built as a prototype by Dearborn Tubing Company (the company that built Fairlane Thunderbolts under contract to Ford), and the remaining ten were built by Holman-Moody in Charlotte, North Carolina. These cars were constructed originally as K-Code (cars equipped with high-performance 289 engines) Mustangs. The cars were taken off the assembly line and had seventeen factory features removed. The parts left off included fenders, glass, bumpers, the engine, the transmission, and the radiator. The bodies were then shipped to Charlotte, where Holman-Moody installed 427-cubic-inch engines.

Ford engineers had developed the single overhead cam (SOHC) 427 to combat Chrysler's Hemi in NASCAR. When NASCAR effectively banned Ford's new engine, the company decided to use it for drag racing. Holman-Moody could secure only seven of the 427 SOHC engines; the other three Mustangs received the high-rise 427 wedge.

These ten Mustangs, which had consecutive VIN numbers, were invoiced to either the dealer or the driver for one dollar each and shipped to drag racers throughout the United States. Gas Rhonda, Dick Brannon, Hubert Platt, and others all raced the new A/FX Mustangs, as did Len Richter, who raced out of Bill Stroppe's Long Beach, California, shop. Richter's A/FX (VIN 5FO9K380237) was the second car built by Holman-Moody. It was originally painted Poppy Red but repainted Champagne Gold for Richter's sponsor, Bob Ford.

Richter entered the car in the 1965 Winternationals, racing his way right up to the finals, where he faced off against the Tasca Ford. His Mustang's axle broke, and victory went to the Tasca car. All during that season, the Mustang's wheels, although remaining stock in dimensions, were pushed forward in relation to the body in order to aid traction by placing the engine's weight closer to the rear axle.

After the 1965 season, and some rules changes in A/FX, Mustang No. 2 was sent back to Charlotte, where Holman-Moody converted it to a 1966 model by placing the wheels back in their original location, then replacing the grille, quarter panels, and other trim items. The car also received a 1966 Holman-Moody ID tag.

After Richter drove it, Jerry Harvey and Hubert Platt raced the Mustang before it was sold to "Dyno Don" Nicholson for the 1969 season. By this time, the four-year-old race car was getting a little long in the tooth as it competed against new cars such as Sox and Martin's Hemi Dart. Still, Nicholson continued to win. The last time Nicholson drove the Mustang was in 1969 at Englishtown, New Jersey. Dyno Don popped the clutch at 9,000 rpms and made it through the traps at 9.89 seconds, setting a new NHRA track record and winning the class for the season.

By the time Nicholson steered the Mustang back to the paddock, men with bags of money were waiting for him. They wanted to buy the car, and they offered him so much money that he couldn't say no.

In the 1960s, there was a strong connection between street drag racers, numbers runners, and drug dealers in the New York area. These dealers took in lots of money—all cash—and needed to find places to spend it. A guy named Tab bought the car from Nicholson and raced it on New York's Connecting Highways and other stretches of straight asphalt against GM and Mopar teams. Rumor has it that Tab would wager as much as $150,000 on a single run. It is said that the Mustang won more than $1 million in one summer from one Chevy team alone!

Eventually, though, the car disappeared.

Curt Vogt was selling telephone systems in 1988 when he heard that Dyno Don's old steed might still exist in the New York area. He had already found and restored another of the eleven original A/FX Mustangs—one that Al

Joniec converted to a stretched-nose Funny Car and campaigned as the *Bat Car*. Vogt savored the thought of another A/FX car—less than fifty miles from his Connecticut home—but he doubted the rumors were true.

"I'd go to all the local swap meets, and I'd talk to guys who said they knew the old Nicholson Mustang was somewhere in New York City," Vogt said. "But I really didn't pay attention because I knew that Nicholson drove Mercurys. Little did I know that he drove this Mustang between his time in Pro-Stock and the Funny Cars.

"When I found out that Nicholson did in fact race a Mustang, I called every speed shop and machine shop in New York City, Brooklyn, Queens, Long Island, and the tri-state area."

Then, one day out of the blue, Vogt got a call from a boisterous Mustang collector named Drake, who said, "Hey, I know where the old Nicholson car is in New York City, but you'll never find it!"

Gold metal flake paint long gone, the once-beautiful drag car fell on hard times when it was nearly forgotten in a Brooklyn storage garage. Gone was the 427 single overhead-cam drivetrain, but the Holman-Moody ID tag and front magnesium wheels were still in place. *Curt Vogt*

"He was bragging and overly confident," Vogt said. "He just knew he'd wind up with the car eventually. I begged him, but when he wouldn't tell me, I stepped up my quest to find the car myself."

Phone call after phone call led to dead ends, but then Vogt had a chance conversation with Long Island engine builder Jack Merkel. Merkel said the Mustang sounded familiar and thought he remembered someone named Lucky once painted the car for a guy named Tab.

Finally, a lead!

Tab was a numbers runner and a drug dealer who was apparently bumped off—dead. But rumors of his death were greatly exaggerated, because he was still alive. But he no longer owned the car. Tab sold it to someone named Tex.

More phone calls revealed a guy named Lucky, who owned an independent towing business in Queens.

"Yeah, I know where it's at," Lucky told Vogt.

"I was on him like a tick," Vogt said. "I dug in and I wouldn't let go. I must have called him two hundred and fifty times over the course of the next year. It took me fifteen months from the time I started looking for the Mustang until I finally had a shot at buying the car."

Vogt hooked onto Lucky and, through him, met his friends Jessie, Three Notes, and Rags. Lucky found Tex, the sixty-year-old street-savvy guy who now owned the Mustang. Tex worked on cars in a dark, dirty one-bay garage and in the street off Myrtle Avenue in Brooklyn.

"I offered Lucky five thousand dollars in cash as a finder's fee," Vogt said. "And I kept fifteen to twenty thousand with me at all times in anticipation of getting a phone call that this car would become available."

"One day he called me and said, 'I think we can buy the car.' I drove to Queens and met at Lucky's apartment.

"I left my pistol at home."

Vogt climbed into Lucky's flatbed truck. Vogt gave Lucky $10,000 in cash. On the way to Brooklyn, they picked up Lucky's friend Bob. Vogt was sweating bullets. He had just handed over a large amount of cash to a stranger, and he was headed for a bad neighborhood and had no idea what would happen next.

"They could have rolled me," Vogt said.

The trio pulled up to Tex's repair shop, and Lucky went inside to try to negotiate a deal. Vogt stayed outside in the truck and talked to Bob.

"He was cool," Vogt said. "He told me a lot of street racing stories."

These negotiations took a couple of hours. Lucky came back out to the truck and said, "Tex said he won't sell the car."

"I gave Lucky another couple of grand, but despite Tex's needy financial condition, he didn't want to sell; it was a no-go," Vogt said.

Frustrated, Vogt drove back home to Connecticut. He was so close to buying a car he had chased for so many months yet so far away.

Then, two weeks later, on June 13, it was ninety-six degrees outside, and Lucky called to report that Tex had changed his mind.

Vogt jumped into his car and hightailed it to Queens. He and Lucky jumped into Lucky's flatbed, and they drove toward Myrtle Avenue, just the two of them.

"It was a real bad area," Vogt said.

When they arrived in Tex's neighborhood, Lucky jumped out of the truck and went in search of Tex. Vogt stayed in the truck. He stuck out like a sore thumb, so he slumped way down in his seat and tried to disappear.

After about a half hour, Lucky returned to the truck without the money. He told Vogt they needed to drive a few blocks away to pick up the car, which he now owned for $11,000, purchased sight unseen. They drove to a garage in a desolate area. Tex opened the garage and there, in the rear of the dusty garage, sat a gray primered Mustang sitting way up in the front, complete with its Holman-Moody ID tag still mounted.

"I had finally found the Holy Grail," Vogt said. "We pushed it into the daylight. It still had its four-inch-wide American racing magnesium front wheels and a parachute with the Ford logo on it."

Lucky and Vogt pushed the Mustang out of the garage and onto Lucky's flatbed, but before they could leave with their booty, they had to pay homage to Tex and his friends in Tex's speakeasy, an after-hours nightclub that he ran up one flight of stairs and down a narrow hallway. The club contained some broken-down pool tables and pinball machines. The two fulfilled their social obligations and left as soon as they could.

Lucky was proud; he showed off the car all over Brooklyn, finally stopping at a speed shop to show his buddies the long-forgotten Mustang.

"I was like a celebrity," Vogt said. "I was in with all the brothers."

Lucky delivered the car to Vogt's house in Connecticut and collected his $5,000. "We unloaded the car in my driveway, shook hands, and said goodbye."

Vogt eventually had the Mustang's body restored by the Super Stang Shop in Lyons, New York, but he supplied the 427 SOHC and drivetrain from his own business, Cobra Automotive.

Having had his fun with the car, and wanting to acquire another car of his dreams (a 427 Cobra), Vogt sold the Mustang A/FX in 1991. He has regretted it ever since.

But he recently received an email from a friend who said he knows a guy whose son bought a 1965 Holman-Moody drag Mustang for $1,200 in the late 1960s.

Maybe it's time for Curt Vogt to pack a briefcase full of cash and find a fresh cast of characters in a shady part of town.

SMOKEY
AND THE BOSS

In the 1960s and 1970s, the SCCA Trans-Am Series had a special sex appeal to car racing fans. Legendary drivers did battle in one of history's most competitive race series, and the cars were the most popular muscle cars ever built.

Late 1960s and early 1970s Camaros, 'Cudas, Challengers, Javelins, and Mustangs were heavily modified by major teams such as Penske or Bud Moore and duked it out on road circuits, such as Laguna Seca, Lime Rock, and Bridgehampton. Those brutal machines are now some of the hottest commodities in the high-priced muscle car collector market.

Friends Ross Myers and Terry Bookheimer have developed a talent for seeking out and purchasing the Ford products that competed in the early SCCA Trans-Am Series. They started buying these cars in the early 1980s, before they became popular, and have since developed quite an impressive vintage racing team. These cars have been restored and race regularly at vintage events throughout the United States.

1970 Boss 302 Mustang
"This was the first car we bought," Bookheimer said. "We both attended Trans-Am races in 1970 and 1971. Ross was into antique cars, but after I told him about the open track days at the Shelby convention, I said, 'Ross, you've got to try this.' So I started to look around for an old race car, even though I didn't know anything about them."

Bookheimer saw a small ad in *Hemmings Motor News* that read "Factory-backed Trans-Am Mustang, One-of-a-kind, Syracuse, New York." He called the phone number and was connected to a bar. Bookheimer thought the bar owner might own the car, but instead, the seller lived above the tavern.

"I'll have him call you back," said the barkeep.

"The guy was a derelict," Bookheimer said. "Finally when he called me back, it was a collect call.

"I negotiated with the guy for six months. Obviously, the market still hadn't caught up with these cars. I drove up to look at it. It had an SCCA brass tag applied to the roll bar but no VIN number.

"'How come there is no serial number?' I asked the seller. 'I don't know,' he said."

Bookheimer soon realized that the reason the seller knew so little about the race car was that he didn't actually own it. He was apparently selling it on spec for the actual owner.

The Mustang was originally built by Ford engineer Ed Hinchliff, whose father was a vice president at Ford. His father was able to secure a bare body-in-white 1970 Mustang for his son to build into a race car. The younger Hinchliff spent all of 1970 building the car into a Trans-Am racer, with help from Ford's factory Trans-Am supplier, Kar Kraft.

This is how Bookheimer discovered the car at a body shop storage yard in New York in June 1983. The car had been stripped of most of its racing goodies, but for a thousand dollars, he feels he got the best of the deal. *Terry Bookheimer*

"Whenever Kar Kraft lunched a motor on the dyno, they'd call Ed and tell him to come and pick it up out of the dumpster," Bookheimer said. "He got all the good parts basically for free."

Hinchliff raced the car in the last two 1970 Trans-Am races and the entire 1971 season.

"He had three top-ten finishes, including a seventh and an eighth, which was quite respectable for a private guy without sponsorship," Bookheimer said.

After the 1971 season, Hinchliff sold the car to Roger Pierce of Syracuse, New York. Pierce raced the car in local SCCA races, but during that time, the car was hit hard in a racing accident. Pierce cosmetically repaired the car and ran it in another couple of races before parking it for good behind a body shop.

"He stripped it for parts and basically junked it," Bookheimer said. "It sat in the storage yard behind the body shop from 1974 until 1981. I was hesitant to buy the car until Pierce told me it was originally Hinchliff's, but after I spoke to him, I decided to buy it."

It was a lucky day for Bookheimer, because not only did he get an authentic Trans-Am Mustang, but Hinchliff still had lots of spare parts for the car—wheels, tires, transmissions, and suspension pieces. And it was all purchased for $1,000.

The car has since been entered in many vintage races, beginning at the 1986 SVRA races at Mid-Ohio.

Now that they've restored it, Myers and Bookheimer regularly compete in vintage Trans-Am events with the car. *Myers/Bookheimer collection*

Smokey's Trans-Am Car

Mechanical wizard Smokey Yunick was well known as a builder of NASCAR stockers and even the occasional Indy car, but most people are not aware Smokey once owned a Trans-Am car. That prize now resides in Myers's and Bookheimer's garage.

The Kar Kraft company of Dearborn, Michigan, built seven Trans-Am Mustangs in 1969: three went to Bud Moore, three went to Carroll Shelby, and one went to Smokey Yunick. Yunick's was built under orders of new Ford president Bunkie Knudsen, who had developed a friendship with Yunick when he ran Pontiac.

"Paint one up for Smokey," said Knudsen, who had Kar Kraft paint one black and gold, the colors Yunick had made famous in Daytona and Indianapolis. It was the only completed car of the seven turned out by Kar Kraft; the rest were sent to Moore and Shelby in only partially completed form. Yunick's car had a completed suspension, was fully wired, and had a race-modified Boss 302 engine, all ready for track action—but Yunick never used the car for Trans-Am racing.

After the car was delivered to Yunick's Daytona Beach shop, he pulled the 302 engine and replaced it with a 427. He and his crew also removed the disc brakes and fitted drums. Yunick was turning the Mustang into a NASCAR Baby Grand stocker for driver Buddy Baker to enter at Talladega.

Baker dominated the first three-quarters of the race until the 427 broke a rocker arm and ended his day. The car never ran in a Trans-Am race.

Yunick sold the car to a Texan, who ran the Mustang as a Modified racer. As such, the doors were hollowed out and welded shut, and a NASCAR roll cage was fitted.

The once-beautiful black-and-gold Boss 302 was used up and put away wet, the fate of many short-track racers. Eventually, it was sold to a man in Houston who collected Boss 302s. It sat in his shed for a number of years.

"Once we got into these Trans-Am cars, we heard about the car's existence through the grapevine," Bookheimer said. "We got a call in 1987 or 1988 from a guy who said that he knew where the seventh Kar Kraft 302 was buried, the old Smokey Yunick car.

"What Smokey Yunick car? Most people didn't even know about the car because it was only driven once and put away. It was forgotten," he added.

Bookheimer went down to Houston to meet the owner, who was a drag racer. He had a drag racing Boss 302 and a concours-restored Boss 302 but didn't have much appreciation for the old racer sitting in his shed. The owner had purchased it cheap in the early 1980s with no intention of restoring it. Bookheimer checked the numbers and the brass Kar Kraft tag that was attached to the roll cage. He negotiated with the man and paid an outrageous price at the time—$20,000.

The car was hauled back to Pennsylvania nonstop on a trailer in thirty-four hours, with Bookheimer and his brother-in-law trading off between sleeping and stints and the wheel.

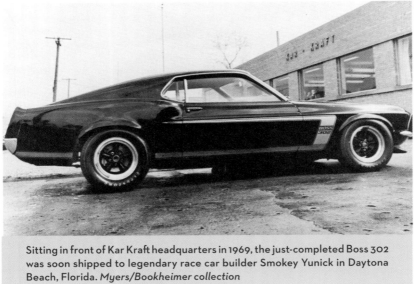

Sitting in front of Kar Kraft headquarters in 1969, the just-completed Boss 302 was soon shipped to legendary race car builder Smokey Yunick in Daytona Beach, Florida. *Myers/Bookheimer collection*

"Thankfully, the car still had many of its original Trans-Am parts: the original Monroe shocks, the trick front A-arms, and the full-floater rear end," he said.

Bookheimer explains that proper Trans-Am cars are easy to identify because they were ordered as Sport Roof Mustangs with 351-cubic-inch engines (which were then swapped for 302s) and no sound-deadening materials. And all the cars had production VIN numbers.

Myers and Bookheimer turned the car over to a top-notch restoration shop in Ohio, the same team that restored Myers's Peter Revson Boss 302 and one of the Penske Javelins. The car was completed in time for the 1995 Monterey Historic races and has been raced regularly since.

"In 1969, these cars ran with dual quads, so the throttle is like an on-off switch," Bookheimer said. "It's a handful."

40-YEAR ITCH TRANS-AM MUSTANG

This 1965 Ford Mustang left the Ford assembly line as a plain Jane six-cylinder coupe, possibly driven out of the showroom by a librarian. But the life it went on to live was far from plain Jane.

Within a year, the Mustang had shed its six-cylinder engine for one of Ford's potent Hi-Po 289s, a four-speed, and a roll bar. Rather than commute to the library, the car regularly did battle on the Sports Car Club of America (SCCA) circuit.

Ray Heppenstall built the Mustang into a race car for amateur racer Buzz Marcus. Marcus entered the car in several SCCA A-Sedan races in 1966, including races held at Watkins Glen, New York, and Reading, Pennsylvania, winning three or four.

The Mustang had been modified with some hard-to-get parts. Instead of Mustang bucket seats, the coupe had black leather seats from a 289 Cobra. It also had a Cobra aluminum T-10 transmission and Carroll Shelby gauges.

Friends George Alderman and Brett Unger were itching to compete at Sebring in SCCA's new Trans-Am series for midsize sedans, but neither one of them owned a suitable car.

"Brett was in military service at the time but thought he would be able to get off from time to time to race," said Alderman. "So we decided, 'Let's go to Sebring!' So I called Buzz [Marcus] and we bought the car from him."

Alderman was a busy man, because around the same time, 1966, in Wilmington, Delaware, he opened one of the first Datsun dealerships in the country, and a year later, he opened a Lotus franchise. In racing, Alderman drove everything from Formula Juniors to McLaren Can-Am cars during his long road racing career.

Maybe because he had raced so many British cars prior to the Mustang, he repainted the Caspian Blue coupe in British Racing Green. Alderman says that he believes the car still had a standard Hi-Po 289 with a single four-barrel carburetor that pulled cool air in from a modified cowl vent. In 1967, fuel cells were not required, so two Mustang gas tanks were split at the seams and the two larger sides were welded together, which gave it a much larger fuel capacity.

"Brett [Unger] couldn't get off for the Sebring races, so Bill Blankenship, who was working for me at the time, was signed on to be my codriver at the Sebring four-hour Trans-Am race," Alderman said. "I came into the pits for fuel and a driver change, but Bill didn't even have his driver's suit on, so I just jumped back in and drove the rest of the race. I finished ninth." He also raced the car at Marlboro and Reading but sold it to Norm Taylor in 1969.

Alderman went on to race additional races with Unger in a Lotus 23, then switched to Datsun 510s and Z-cars in IMSA, where he won the 1971 and 1974 Baby Grand Championships.

In January 2009, Alderman, his son, Paul, and restoration friend Erich Bollman repurchased the car. They intend to restore it to its 1967 Trans-Am livery and begin vintage racing it. *George Alderman collection*

Alderman all but forgot about the old Mustang until forty years later, when his son, Paul, began racing and restoring old Mustangs. Taylor, who entered the car in a driver's school at Marlboro and street raced the Mustang, eventually parked the tired old racer under a lean-to in the back lot of his commercial water business.

"I talked to Norm [Taylor] and his wife about twenty years ago to see if I could buy the car," Paul Alderman said. "I was told no and not to call again. But I knew one of their employees, and he told me the car was still there."

When Taylor died in the fall of 2008, a deal was agreed upon over a three-month period through a mutual friend, Bob Burris. But the deal nearly went awry.

"One of the Taylor's employees decided to clean up the storage yard after Norm died," Paul said. "There was a bunch of old trailers, an old Impala, and the Mustang. He decided to haul them all to the junkyard.

"We had to race to the junkyard to retrieve it before it got crushed. We never got to inspect the trailers, which we think had some of the original parts the car was missing, like the engine and the radiator."

But at least they had George's old race car back. These days, the Aldermans own an automotive machine shop, having sold the Datsun/Nissan dealership several years ago. Certainly they can handle the rebuilding of the drivetrain, but restoration of the body, which had deteriorated badly, would require a pro. So the Aldermans made Erich Bollman, owner of Christiana Muscle Car Restoration, a partner in the car.

Paul and Erich hope to take turns racing the car in vintage sports car races when it is competed.

"It was such a neutral car to drive," said George. "I was always right up there with the Corvettes when I raced it in A-Sedan."

A happy reunion, forty years later.

THEY CALL IT THE
MOTOWN MISSILE

For a young Eara Merritt, one *Hot Rod Magazine* image stands out more than any other: that of the Pro Stock driver Don Carleton launching the *Motown Missile* from the starting line at the 1972 Pomona Nationals, wheels reaching for the sky. It was an iconic image that stayed with Merritt throughout his adult life.

But his automotive interests didn't favor Chrysler products. Merritt liked Fords, especially Shelby products. "I used to go to all the Shelby conventions in the early days," said the retired civil and mechanical engineer. "That's where I met Mark Williamson and his brother Dan, two straggly guys from Canada who used to hang around with me at those Shelby meets."

Like Merritt, Mark Williamson fell in love with Shelby Mustangs but never seemed to have enough money to purchase one. "I'd see Mark at Shelby meets year after year, and we became friends," Merritt said.

"One day in 1983 or '84, he called and said he found an old race car that quite possibly could have been the original *Motown Missile*. It was for sale for five thousand dollars, and he wanted my advice on the car's value. I told him to buy it, then we lost track of each other for the next twenty years."

In 2007, though, Williamson called Merritt and asked if he'd like to ride to Amelia Island Concours d'Elegance with him. "Of course!" Merritt said.

En route to Florida, Merritt asked, "What ever happened to that old 'Cuda drag car you bought?"

"Oh," Williamson said, "it's sitting in my backyard." Merritt almost had a stroke. The image of the wheel-standing *Motown Missile* from *Hot Rod* Magazine from

By being nice to a couple of Canadian vintage car enthusiasts, Merritt was able to negotiate a transfer of ownership for a wheel-standing factory 'Cuda. Merritt had the car brought from Ottawa to a restoration shop near Jackson, Mississippi. *Eara Merritt*

forty years earlier came to mind. Williamson showed him a photograph of the decrepit race car, which had sat beside his house for the past twenty years.

It was too much. "How about selling it to me?" Merritt asked.

"I'll think about it," Williamson said.

One year went by, then two. Finally, in 2010, Merritt made Williamson an offer: "Mark, I'll pay for the restoration, and we'll be partners in the car." Williamson agreed.

The car was moved from Ottawa to Star, Mississippi, and into Paul's Body Shop, Merritt's favorite restoration garage. And there it sat for two years as they researched, documented, and collected the right parts to complete the restoration. Merritt even had the car's original car builder, Dick Oldfield, verify that the car was the authentic *Motown Missile*.

In 2012, the car went into "full restoration mode," according to Merritt. It was dipped in acid for the second time in its life; when it was new, it had been dipped first to make it lighter for drag racing, and now it was dipped again to remove decades of rust and corrosion.

The restoration took a sabbatical for a little while in 2012, when it was brought to the annual East Coast Drag Racing Hall of Fame in Henderson, North Carolina. There it was united with the three other *Motown Missiles* that were built and raced from 1970 to 1972.

"It was just out of the dip-tank, and it looked like the photos of the car when it was first built in 1971," Merritt said. "This was a bonafide Chrysler factory race car that was built to make the Hemi the dominant engine in drag racing."

The rest, as they say, is history.

A CLASSIC ON CRAIGSLIST: LAGONDA

BY STEVE SILVERSTEIN

I had never looked at the Craigslist website. In fact, I was only prompted to check it out when a friend at work mentioned he had once bought a cheap chainsaw on the site.

So that evening I went home and found the Boston link for Craigslist. And being a typical car person, I typed "race car" in the search bar. About three items down, a listing read, "1939 Lagonda Le Mans, raced by John Fitch." That was all it said.

At that moment, a lot of things ran through my head. First was, "This has to be a joke." Next was, "Who in the world would list a Lagonda Le Mans on Craigslist?"

As I clicked on the heading, sure enough, up popped a photo of an enormous body, in sections, lying by the woodpile. It was an old photo—a moment frozen in time. A little shocked, I sat and contemplated the ad.

Naturally, I called. Since it was Thursday, I explained that I wouldn't be able to look at the car until Saturday morning. Amazingly, it was in Lexington, Massachusetts, near my home. Complicating matters, though, I was supposed to pick up my mother, who was due to arrive at Boston's Logan Airport that

The Lagonda at the Seneca Cup races at Watkins Glen in 1952, where it was driven by Sherwood Johnson to a first in Class, third Overall finish. The car was now owned by Gary Fuller. *Steve Silverstein collection*

morning. My mother is a sport, even though she just doesn't have much of an appreciation for old cars. Particularly, old cars in crappy barns.

As my mother and I were driving down the Mass Pike heading home, I explained I would have to make a detour to what had to be one of the last working farms in Lexington. Upon arrival, I pulled into the driveway, and there, sitting at the entrance of the barn, was indeed an old body. I can assure you my mother wasn't impressed.

As I talked with the owner, he explained that his father had taken the body off of the original chassis in the late fifties. From there, the body was stored in the rafters, for all these years. There were many parts, but no chassis.

I started to realize that this was probably a very historically significant car, but I'm no Lagonda expert and certainly not well versed in the history. I asked what happened to the chassis, and the owner explained he didn't know. I wanted to be honest with the owner, and after talking with him, I explained if he had the chassis, the car could be worth tens of thousands, if not hundreds of thousands, of dollars as is.

His father was still alive and his mother was still alive, but separated, so I asked him to inquire if they could remember what happened to the chassis. At the same time, my head was swiveling around looking for a "Lagonda" farm wagon behind the barn. Regardless, I explained I really wanted what he had and I'd touch base with him to see if he found more information on the chassis.

An amazing barn-find discovery, the body of the historic Lagonda race car spread out on new owner Steve Silverstein's Massachusetts front yard. *Steve Silverstein collection*

The body of the same car mounted on a display frame. Steve's son, David, poses next to his father's new acquisition. *Steve Silverstein collection*

For the next two months, I'd call, but he hadn't had a chance to talk with his parents. Finally, after about the fifth call, he said, "My father said the chassis was scrapped. If you want it make an offer, you can; otherwise, I'm selling it to a kid down the road who wants to put it on a VW chassis." Of course, I bought it.

That night I received a call from Jim Donick, who is a good friend in the Vintage Sports Car Club of America (VSCCA). Jim said, and I may have this quote wrong, "Steve, I know you think you know what you bought, but let me tell you what you really bought."

This is the point where even I couldn't keep up with the car's convoluted history.

Lagonda took a pair of cars to Le Mans in 1939. The company had great success by finishing first and second in class and third and fourth overall. Unfortunately, with World War II starting, the cars were stored at the Lagonda factory, where both were nearly destroyed by a V-1 bomb. The remains of both cars were eventually sold, and one was rebuilt to compete in the 1946 Indy 500.

As history shows, the Lagonda did not qualify for Indy in 1946, though the team tried very hard. After the unsuccessful qualifying effort, the car was intended to return to the UK. Unfortunately, the owner, Robert Arbuthnot, was killed in a car crash shortly after the 1946 Indianapolis event. After that, the Lagonda Le Mans was sold to Dr. Raymond N. Sabourin here in the United States, and drivers such as John Fitch and Sherwood Johnston raced it in many early Sports Car Club of America (SCCA) races and hillclimbs.

The Lagonda's V-12 failed early on, so as the years progressed, it was also powered by a Mercury flathead V-8 and an early Chrysler 331-cubic-inch Hemi.

Fast forward to 1960. The body was removed with the intent of placing a Buick body on the Lagonda chassis, from what I was told. Sometime in the 1960s, the chassis was sold to a Lagonda Club member in New Jersey and then to a museum in Canada, and in the mid-1980s, it returned to England for rebuilding.

Finally, in 2008, I was staring at the Lagonda body in my yard and lots of miscellaneous parts. I intended to hang the body from the vaulted ceiling in my den as a piece of auto art. Well, once together, I realized how imposing this enormous car really was. The den is big . . . but not that big.

Eventually, the original chassis—number 14090, now looking splendid with a new Frank Feeley body—came up for auction in 2012, and I always had visions of the Indy body being preserved by the current or even the future owner of the original chassis. However, that really didn't work out either. After years of ownership, I sold the body to a man in Germany.

VERITAS BMW

Heath Rodney and his business partner Derrick Freshour are both car enthusiasts, and because they grew up in Middle America, Iowa, it's not surprising
their interests run toward high-performance American cars. Certainly not
imported cars.

"We're basically muscle car guys—Trans Ams, GTOs, that kind of thing,"
said Rodney, who today owns the Indian motorcycle franchise in Sturgis,
South Dakota.

"We grew up in Villisca, Iowa, a small town of twelve hundred people," he
added. "Everyone knew everyone, and they all knew that Derrick and I were
car guys."

In January 2017, Freshour got a phone call from the owner of an old car in
Council Bluffs, about twenty miles from Villisca.

"I have a 1950 BMW in my barn, and I'm in the process of downsizing," said
the older gentleman, eighty-seven, who was in the process of selling his farm
and moving to Texas.

Neither Rodney nor Freshour got very excited. After all, it was a sixty-year-old
German car, a brand that neither had any particular interest in. Still, it was a
vintage car that some enthusiast might be interested in purchasing.

The owner didn't mention the car was actually a Veritas.

"We got the call one day and picked it up the next day," Rodney said.

Even though neither had much knowledge about BMWs, this one looked
special. It was rusty, yes, and sitting in the corner of a barn. But it didn't look

Nesting between farm implements, a tractor, and the wall, the BMW Veritas was protected from the elements but not the bird droppings. *Heath Rodney*

like any BMW Rodney or Freshour had ever seen. It was a two-seater and had a sporty profile.

Rodney and Freshour began putting out feelers in an effort to identify their new asset. They contacted the archives department at BMW in Munich, Germany, but couldn't get much information there. Finally, they connected with BMW expert Jim Profitt, who specializes in 328 models. Profitt was instantly interested.

"Take the radiator out and tell me what the serial number is directly below the radiator," he told Rodney and Freshour. A couple of days later, they gave Profitt the information he requested.

"You have no idea what you just found."

Rodney and Freshour had stumbled across the thirty-first BMW 328 sports car, one that had been extensively raced throughout Europe before World War II.

"Your chassis, number eight-five-zero-three-one, was one of the first three sports cars delivered to BMW's racing department," Profitt said.

The two friends were confused. They were told this was a 1950 BMW, yet it was raced in Europe a decade earlier. And how did such a car wind up in rural Iowa?

The two muscle car enthusiasts were about to become BMW historians.

Let's go back to 1937, when the chassis for this stylish, albeit rusty, coupe was manufactured. By the time this car was built, the two other German auto manufacturers—Mercedes-Benz and Auto Union (Audi)—were already seriously involved in Grand Prix. BMW also sought to gain international exposure through racing, so three chassis were sent to the competition department for modification.

The standard 80-horsepower, two-liter, six-cylinder engine was modified by BMW engineers to reach between 130 and 136 horsepower. Externally, a belly pan was added for improved aerodynamics, and the bucket seats were made thinner and lighter.

Even without these modifications, the 328 was already winning its share of races. With them, the car was dominant in the two-liter class and even in larger displacement groups.

In addition to scores of less-prestigious races, chassis number 85031 competed in 1937 in the 24 Hours of Le Mans and won the RAC Tourist Trophy. In 1938, it competed again in the RAC Tourist Trophy race and Mille Miglia.

With the onset of World War II, BMW scaled back its racing program, and the 328 racers were put in storage. Surprisingly, many survived the war. When the war ended, the 328s were either sold to privateers or given to BMW engineers in lieu of unpaid salaries. This chassis was one of those that survived.

When peace was restored in Europe, three former BMW racing engineers began a company called Veritas. The new company rebodied BMWs with aerodynamic, envelope bodies and sold them as new cars for racing and road use.

The history of chassis number 85031 goes dark from 1950 until it materialized in an Iowa barn in 2017.

"The gentleman we bought the car from said he bought it as a non-running car in 1971," Rodney said. "He didn't remember who he purchased it from. So we can't verify how it came to the States or how it wound up on an Iowa farm."

Rodney and Freshour have traveled to BMW headquarters in Munich, Germany, to conduct additional research on the car.

"BMW wanted to restore the car for us," Rodney said. "Now the car is a big deal to them. But BMW wouldn't actually perform the restoration themselves, but instead contract it out."

So the partners will do their own restoration.

"It will take a couple of years," Rodney said. "We've completely disassembled the car and have contracted with one of the top restoration shops to assist us."

So far, the engine has been removed, crated, and sent to Europe for a rebuild. And Rodney and Freshour have contracted with a body company in Europe to fabricate a new 328 body so that when restored, it will look like it did in its racing form in 1937.

"We're restoring it as a race car and hope to take it to the Pebble Beach Concours when it is finished," Rodney said.

But what about the unique and potentially beautiful Veritas body that was installed in 1950? What will happen to that?

Rodney and Freshour have that figured out. They will mount the body on a spare BMW tube frame the pair has already located.

Rodney admits that as muscle car enthusiasts, they are playing in an automotive arena in which they have little knowledge. But they are taking advice from some of the top BMW restorers in the world.

"We're basically Budweiser guys building a car for Pebble Beach," he said.

Oh, and Rodney adds that the two beer drinkers are no longer neophytes in the world of historic European cars. Through their research, they discovered that another BMW Veritas roadster once lived about a hundred miles away in Lincoln, Nebraska.

BMW #85031 is currently undergoing a thorough restoration, with the guidance of BMW experts, to bring it back to its 1937 level of racing preparation. *Heath Rodney*

"We were told it was brought back from Europe by an American GI in 1951 or '52," Rodney explained. "In the seventies, it had a small-block Chevy installed. It was sold sometime in the eighties.

"We figure the same GI probably brought the two Veritases, ours and the one in Lincoln, back from Europe at the same time. I mean, what are the chances of two similar cars so close to each other in the Midwest?

"It's just too much of a coincidence."

RARITIES AND ODDBALLS

THE ABARTH BIPOSTO

BY RICK CAREY

Miles Morris, then head of Christie's International Motor Cars Department, called in the late spring of 2003.

"Rick," he said, "I wonder if you'd do a little job for us." I'd written auction catalog descriptions for Miles, his colleague Malcolm Welford, and their predecessor at Christie's, David Gooding, so this wasn't out of the ordinary—yet a little early for Christie's next motor cars auction at Rockefeller Center in early June. "We're consigning a car that's been sitting for about thirty years in a barn up near you, and I wonder if you'd be willing to go over, air up the tires, push it outside, take some photos, and write the catalog description."

Fortunately, the answer to my first question, "Do I get paid?" was affirmative. So I said, "Sure. Where is it, and what's the car?" figuring it was something interesting but mundane, such as a tired old XK120, early Corvette, or Bentley Mark VI. "Well," Miles responded, "it's in an estate and we don't have all the papers signed yet so I can't really tell you, but you'll like it . . . a lot."

Ten days later, he called back. "The papers are signed and you can go see the car. Here's the name of the neighbor who's looking after the late owner's house. He has keys, will give you directions, and can let you in. The car is pretty interesting."

Tease.

"It's a 1952 Abarth 1500 with one-off Bertone coachwork designed by Franco Scaglione that was displayed at the Turin Motor Show."

Let's see, that's 1) a very early Abarth; 2) with one-off bodywork; 3) an auto show display car; and 4) designed by Franco Scaglione. Scaglione was a brilliant but low-profile designer, creator of the three Alfa Romeo BATs, extravagant aerodynamic experiments with pointed noses and curved fins that shocked the auto styling world in the mid-1950s. Franco Scaglione is one of my heroes.

I was up out of my chair in an instant, still on the phone but also pulling Abarth, Bertone, and coachwork reference books off the shelf. There it was, in each of the books, in period black-and-white shots from the Turin Auto Show, each with the same story: the first Scaglione design for Bertone, selected as the "Most Outstanding Car" at Turin in 1952, sold off the show stand to Packard and shipped to the states, subsequent history unknown.

This was no ordinary car. This was the answer to a half-century-old mystery.

Moments after hanging up with Miles, I was talking with his contact and arranging to visit first thing the next morning to assess the Abarth's condition. The rest of the evening was spent researching and wondering.

I found that Peter Vack, author of *The Illustrated Abarth Buyer's Guide*, believes the Abarth 1500 Biposto is the first Fiat-based Abarth, the cornerstone of a long and illustrious collaboration between the Austrian-born Carlo Abarth and Fiat. Based on the short-lived Fiat 1400 platform and bearing typical Abarth tuning tweaks like free-flow exhaust and a pair of Weber Tipo 36 downdraft

Built by Franco Scaglione for the 1952 Turin Motor Show, this car resided in a proper three-car garage just three miles from Carey's Connecticut home for more than thirty years. *Rick Carey*

carburetors, its short-stroke four-cylinder engine was a much better basis for Scaglione's aerodynamic interpretations than the tall, long-stroke Alfa Romeo 1900s upon which the BATs were built.

It has all the elements of a BAT (the acronym stands for Berlina Aerodinamica Technica): a large central headlight flanked by grilles and peaked front fenders with smaller headlights; a light and graceful roof with raked windshield and side glass; a central spline down the rear glass; cutaway wheelwells; and delicate, intricately sculpted rear fender fins that gently urge airflow back across the rear deck to merge with the flow over the roof.

Scaglione had no wind tunnel. His aerodynamics were intuitive, a visually pleasing expression of fluid flow around a solid object that had to include practical elements, such as wheels, radiators, occupants, and windows. They are sensual without being voluptuous, implicitly effective without artifice. The 1952 Abarth 1500 Bertone Biposto is one of the cornerstones of aerodynamic automobile design.

How could such a significant—and visually striking—car have simply disappeared for fifty years, yet survive in, I was told, sound, complete, and nearly original condition? Subsequent research, with invaluable help from the archivists at *Fortune* magazine, revealed the story.

Bill Graves, Packard's engineering vice president, and Edward Macauley, its chief designer, had gone to Turin in 1952 looking for design ideas to freshen up Packard's bulky postwar cars. They weren't successful, but they were so struck by the Abarth Biposto that they bought it and brought it back to the United States in hopes that it would provide some inspiration. Their quest didn't succeed. However, in 1952, a young *Fortune* writer, Richard Austin Smith, came to Detroit to write a story about Packard's prospects under its new president, James C. Nance, recently brought in from GE's Hotpoint appliance division

Smith saw the Abarth and was intrigued with it, even recounting its story in his article and using it as the setting for a photo of Packard executives in which Nance was quoted describing its style as "lunar asparagus." During the visit, Smith also offered some suggestions for advertising slogans while meeting with Packard's advertising VP.

After they were picked up and used, Nance wrote to Smith, offering to pay him for his creativity. Smith responded that as a *Fortune* employee, he couldn't accept payment from the subject of an article, whereupon Nance proposed to give him "the Abarth foreign car . . . to compensate you even though I know that the assistance you gave us was not done with this in mind." He also reminded Smith that he'd have to pay taxes on the Abarth's value

This Biposto two-seater was purchased by Packard's engineering and styling department to provide the company with inspiration for future models. *Rick Carey*

on Packard's books: $100. The original letters were in Richard Smith's files. Nance's letter offering to give the Abarth to Smith bore the approval initials of *Fortune*'s senior editors, along with a short note, "Enjoy the car."

He apparently did, because he preserved it carefully even while driving it enough that its odometer showed 31,926 kilometers. His children remembered their father picking them up at school in the Abarth and being the center of attention when he did. Some years later, he and his wife retired to an eighteenth-century farmhouse on the eastern Connecticut shoreline. They built a new, tight three-car garage and thirty years ago drove the Abarth Biposto into the center stall, where it stayed until 2003.

We opened the garage door early on a cold and dreary New England April morning. There sat the Biposto, dusty and neglected, but miraculously complete. I think I entered a zone walking around it, translating the few photographic images into impressions of the real thing, the genuine article. Unseen by the world at large for a half-century, there it was, carefully and so obviously lovingly preserved by Richard Smith, a hundred-dollar car that was so much more. Richard Smith was no megabuck collector with a barn full of treasures. He wasn't even a hoarder, buying up neglected hulks in the hope they'd someday fund a lavish retirement. He had two cars in his garage: the Abarth Biposto and a 1998 Ford Taurus.

A few days later, we came back to take photos. The weather was still crummy, with snow lingering in the bushes and the ground sodden over a layer of frost. A cedar tree had grown up outside the garage, and the Abarth's brakes were stiff. Even four of us could barely push it outside, and it was a tight fit between the cedar and the garage door. We didn't even think to maneuver the Biposto into a more photogenic location. All we wanted was to take some documentary shots, then push it back inside and go get a cup of hot coffee, which we did.

Pushed onto a rollback in early June for the trip to New York and Christie's auction, the Biposto got its first "wash" in a generation. A chill rain fell on Rockefeller Center for the preview and Miles Morris's presentation of the Abarth to NBC's *The Today Show* audience. At the preview on Wednesday evening, lubricated by complimentary Cosmopolitans swirling through ice sculptures, a pool developed. It was a buck a person; seventeen dollars was collected.

The dealers and collectors there for the Biposto were assiduous in their assessment: a hundred thousand dollars, give or take. They were voting with their pocketbooks, not their aspirations, hoping to buy for a buck and sell for a buck-twenty-five. Others were more enthusiastic, or perhaps more Cosmopolitan. The top estimate? It was $275,000 against Christie's high estimate of $120,000.

The dealers never got their hands out of their pocketbooks because the Biposto surged right through Christie's estimate in a heartbeat and eventually sold to a phone bidder from England for a hammer bid of $260,000, a final price of $293,500 with Christie's buyer's commission. It wasn't the top sale of the evening—a Delage D8120 Cabriolet Grand Sport at $656,500 took those honors—but it was definitely the star of the show.

Now being restored in England, the Abarth 1500 Bertone Biposto is on anyone's list of the great barn finds of the first decade of this century, and it demonstrates that there really are great, wonderful, important, and beautiful cars out there waiting to be discovered. This one was in a garage in Groton, Connecticut, only about three miles from my home.

FROM BEHIND THE
IRON CURTAIN

Along with its greater horrors, World War II destroyed objects of beauty beyond counting. Many rare and fascinating cars were lost to the ravages of warfare; others were confiscated and used to transport officers, and most of those disappeared too. A few, such as the Paris-Salon Delahaye model 135M profiled here, survived into the twenty-first century through a combination of careful planning and luck.

The car was built for a Bohemian businessman named Adamek in 1937. He had seen a similar car at the Paris Automobile Show the previous year. That car, with coachwork by Figoni et Falaschi of Paris's Boulougne-sur-Seine area, sold to Indian Prince Aly Khan for the incredible price of $27,000 US dollars. Mr. Adamek wanted a car like it with the same company's coachwork.

He placed his order through the Vienna Delahaye agent, Hoffman and Hupport, for a 1937 model. The Delahaye company obliged by manufacturing Competition Chassis number 48666 and shipping it off to Figoni et Falaschi. The coachbuilder installed body number 676, a short wheelbase "Competition Court," or "Roadster Grand Sport," model. The car was painted an elegant *"gris lumière et rouge foncé"*—a very light gray with deep red trim.

When the war started, Adamek had the foresight to hide the car, which protected it from confiscation. After the war, the Delahaye number 48666 was resurrected and driven throughout northern Bohemia through the 1950s and 1960s. Records suggest that it was once raced on an amateur level during its life in Czechoslovakia.

In 1969, the fabulous Delahaye, like so many cars before it and after, found its way into a barn. The man who bought it intended to restore it, but he never found the time. For the next three decades, the Delahaye sat disassembled in a barn just outside Prague, its Figoni et Falaschi coachwork and other parts hanging from the walls. Its owner knew the car's value and had some idea on whom to get word to when he decided to sell. That word reached Jacques Harguindeguy through a Delahaye parts seller he liked to spend time with at Retromobile, Paris's week-long parts swap meet.

Shortly after the 1997 Retromobile, that friend called Harguindeguy with a unique opportunity: a sixty-year-old Delahaye, disassembled and concealed for half its life in a Prague barn, was up for sale. "When he described the car to me, I told him that I would give my balls for a car like that," Harguindeguy said. "He said that nobody else knew about this car, but I only had three days to give him my decision."

That was Friday, so Harguindeguy asked for, and thankfully received, two extra days, so he could investigate the car among French collectors. "On Monday, I got hold of the archivist for the Delahaye club in France," he said. "He actually knew about the car but said the old gentleman who owned it wanted two hundred fifty thousand dollars for it, which, in his mind, was way too much money. I was very nervous, because there are lots of fake ones around. He told me that even though it was in poor condition and disassembled, it was authentic."

Harguindeguy had another friend, Christoph Grohe of Switzerland, travel to Prague to see the car in person. Before he arrived in Prague, Grohe was suspicious that the car might be a replica. But upon seeing the car, and discovering that the Figoni et Falaschi body was indeed genuine, he knew that he was in the presence of a very special car. Even though it was disassembled, the car showed traces of its original pearl-gray paint, dark red accents, and red leather interior. The car seemed to be complete but was missing its cosmetic chrome trim and a radiator.

"I said, 'Thank you very much,' and bought the car," Harguindeguy said. "I was amazed that even though the car was apart and had been neglected for decades, the original engine with the correct number 37 stamping was still with the car. This was rare."

Harguindeguy had struck a deal, but the purchase was only a step in getting the car. Next came the tricky business of removing it from the Czech Republic. "The car was totally in pieces, so we had to pay lots of under-the-table money to government officials to get it out of the country," he said. "When

Assembly before Shiping in Switzerland. Aug 1997 —

Having made it through the war, the Delahaye, then in Czechoslovakia, was raced for a while, then disassembled for a restoration that was never completed. Here, the car is bolted together for shipment to the United States in 1997. *Jacques Harguindeguy*

it arrived in Switzerland, I had the car loosely assembled so it would fit into a shipping container."

The car was then shipped to Harguindeguy's California home in 1998. Restoration began in March 1999, and it took approximately two years to complete. He worked closely with Brian Hoyt of Perfect Reflections in Haywood, California, whose shop restored the car as Harguindeguy conducted research and sourced parts. "The engine block was in very bad shape," he said. "It had frozen and was cracked, but we saved it. I bought three Delahayes to restore this one."

One of the toughest jobs was recasting the elegant brightwork that runs around the headlights and taillights and the trim on the fenders. Using only blurry prewar photos of his car and other Figoni et Falaschi models of the era, Harguindeguy and his restorers exquisitely reproduced the trim in solid brass before sending it to the platers.

Harguindeguy received the car from the restoration shop in July 2000, when he brought it to the upholstery shop to have its unique bench front-seat interior trimmed. One month later, he trailered the Delahaye to Pebble Beach for the annual Concours d'Elegance. In contrast to most of the other owners of classic cars, though, he didn't show the car to anyone during the days leading up to the Sunday classic. "I kept the car hidden in my trailer prior to the show," he said, not wanting the politics of car judging to "predetermine" his car before the show.

By coincidence, Claude Figoni, son of the cofounder of the famous Figoni et Falaschi coach-building team, was invited in 2000 to Pebble Beach as grand marshal. "I only showed Claude the car in the trailer on Saturday, and a little tear came to his eye," Harguindeguy said. "He said it looked like it left our shop yesterday."

Early on Sunday morning of the fiftieth Pebble Beach event, Harguindeguy opened the trailer, backed his car out, and drove it toward the legions of car fans and the judges. The crowd was floored by the car's beauty, its elegant lines, and beautiful details. Clearly the car was a show favorite, but Harguindeguy wouldn't know which car won the coveted Best of Show until all the award winners were driven across the judging stand. As he and his daughter, Debbie Wall, drove the Delahaye across the stand, in front of the thousands of spectators, a confetti cannon exploded and rained colored ribbons on his car. Harguindeguy had won the most prestigious award in the world of car collectors.

The Delahaye that survived the war, some amateur racing, and a long stint scattered about a Czech barn was finally recognized as the best in the world. Once more, it boasted the beauty and artistry with which it entered the world in an earlier century. But additional showings of the car was of no interest to Harguindeguy. "It's already won the biggest award in the world," he said. "What could be better than that?"

SLEEPING BEAUTIES

REPRINTED WITH PERMISSION
FROM *AUTOMOBILE QUARTERLY*, VOL. 22, NO. 2

I read the following story in Automobile Quarterly when it was published in the early 1980s. I was intrigued with the almost perverted beauty of these rotting classics. It started me thinking that maybe not every Bugatti or Cord needs to be restored, but maybe every once in a while, a car of this sort should be allowed to slowly return to dust. I fell in love with these photographs and couldn't stop looking at every detail: the moss growing on the Alfa Romeo, the dandelion growing from the Lancia windowsill. A poster series was offered by Automobile Quarterly, which I desperately wanted. But at the time, money was tight, and I couldn't justify the purchase. Today, a quarter-century later, I'd still love to find a set of those posters to surround myself with these incredible "Sleeping Beauties."

I saved the story as my all-time favorite "barn-find piece," and its imagery helped to inspire this book. Though the cars it describes may be out of reach, there's something optimistic here too—a link from present to past and a sense of the automobile's organic place in our lives.

I am so thankful that the fine folks at Automobile Quarterly have allowed this story and a couple of the photographs to appear again.

—TOM COTTER

"If only . . ." One leans back and imagines all the lost opportunities in life. A lover long since departed, but never forgotten. The job offer refused. The letter left unsent. Of course, there is nothing to be done; the vile worm of time continues inexorably forward. And yet someone or something has given us the terrible gift of nostalgia. "If only . . ."

From left: Cord 812, ca. 1937; Bugatti Type 57 coupe, ca. 1935–1938; Bugatti Type 5 coupe, ca. 1932–1935. *Herbert W. Hesselmann*

A casual glance at the classifieds of just a decade ago reveals some bleak realities about missed opportunities. A Cobra goes begging for $12,000, a Ferrari Lusso seeks a buyer at only $8,500, a Corvette for a song, a Jaguar for a pittance. During the Depression, it must have been even worse as the vanquished playboys resigned their elegant playthings for a fistful of bills. Though the dollars they sought were much more powerful than those of the present day, the prices they asked are still low enough to make us weep. "If only . . ."

The photographs on these pages are yet another case in point. Rusting, rotting, and decaying, these "sleeping beauties" will never be awakened by the restorer's kiss. Their owner has acquired them as if they were stray cats, unwanted and unloved. For most, he paid practically nothing. Some were even gifts. And none will ever be sold.

We cannot tell you the precise location of this sirens' graveyard. We know only that it is located somewhere in Europe. German photographer Herbert Hesselmann is one of the lucky who have been allowed to enter this hallowed crypt.

Though worthy of poetry, we present these death masks with identification but without comment. Many of the faces are familiar, most would be priceless if restored today. Yet they lie sleeping peacefully, perhaps forever.

Jowett Javelin, ca. 1952 (front); Alfa Romeo Type 6C2500 C, ca. 1948–1950 (left), which ran in the 1950 Mille Miglia and Targa Florio and is one of three built; Bugatti "Fiacre" Type 44, ca. 1927, is on the right.
Herbert W. Hesselmann

LENO'S DUESIES

Duesenbergs are very, very rare. For example, Ford built fifteen million Ford Model Ts, while Duesenberg built a total of 481 Model J, SJ, and JN cars during the Depression era of 1928 to 1937.

Duesenbergs were also very expensive.

When a new Ford Model A roadster could be had for $380, Duesies sold for between $16,000 and $25,000, even more for a few cars with custom coachwork.

"People who bought these cars new were Fortune 500–type guys," said Randy Ema of Orange, California. Ema is a Duesenberg expert. He's also the guy Duesenberg enthusiast Jay Leno relies on for advice on his favorite brand of car.

When Duesenbergs were built, they were without question the finest cars in the world, surpassing Rolls-Royce, Mercedes, and Hispano-Suiza in power, ride, and technical sophistication. In the 1930s, an unsupercharged Model J produced a claimed 265 horsepower from its twin-cam, thirty-two-valve straight-eight engine—quite a lot when Ford V-8s of the same era, considered powerhouses, produced just 85 horsepower.

The most advanced cars built at the time, Duesenbergs were packed with innovative features, including a self-lubrication feature on the Model J. Owners included kings, princes, gangsters, religious leaders, and celebrities such as William Randolph Hearst, Howard Hughes, Gary Cooper, and Clark Gable.

And now Jay Leno.

In addition to nearly a hundred other interesting cars, Leno owns several Duesenbergs, and he is somewhat of an authority on the marque. So when he heard about a couple of "forgotten" Duesenbergs, he was all ears.

1927 Duesenberg Model X

"When people see me on TV and learn that I'm a car collector, they want me to see their cars," said the former host of NBC's *The Tonight Show.*

"Sometimes they want me to own their cars."

Such was the case with the 1927 Duesenberg Model X garaged in Burbank, California, just a few miles from the NBC Studios where Leno used to work each day.

"This guy named Harry owned a garage and was a race car enthusiast," Leno said. "He bought this old Duesenberg for three hundred dollars out of Chicago back in 1946, probably with the intention of restoring it."

Harry had the car transported to California on a train. Because his purchase had a blown engine, Harry tied a chain around his car's bumper and towed the Duesenberg from the station to his house in Burbank.

He put it in his garage behind the house, locked the door, and didn't open it again for almost sixty years.

"I always knew Harry had something interesting in his garage," Leno said. "He had a Duesenberg racing engine that had won at Indianapolis stored in a box in his yard. But he'd never let me inside the garage.

"I'd drive by his house with my Stanley Steamer, blow the horn—beep-beep—and take him for a ride around town. But still he kept the contents of the garage a secret.

"'Hey, Harry, what's in the garage?' I'd say. 'Wouldn't you like to know,' is all he'd answer."

But when Harry was ninety-two years old and about to enter a nursing home, he called Leno and said he could go into the garage—which was no easy task, since earthquakes over the years had made the doors almost impossible to open.

When Leno and his friend Randy Ema finally got inside, it was like he was walking into a time capsule.

"There were newspapers stacked up in there with news about the end of World War II," Leno said. "There were Orange Crush soda cans and old porcelain signs from the era."

According to Ema, thirteen Model Xs were built, and four exist today.

"It was nice enough but had a worn-out engine," Ema said.

"Thank goodness Harry left the windows closed, so there were no moths or mice in the interior."

Harry had had a change of heart, and now he wanted Leno to own the car. Leno negotiated with Harry's daughter, who, although she lived in the house nearly all her life, knew nothing of the prestigious car in the backyard garage. Leno wanted the car, but wanted to be fair about the price, so he suggested that the family have appraisers come in and determine a price. Leno agreed with their price, and he made the purchase, not only of the Model X, but the entire contents of the garage.

"I bought all sorts of neat items—the signs, old parts," he said.

"There was also another Duesenberg in the garage, a Model A that had been hacked up with some kind of Packard body."

The Model X car was in good enough condition when it was pulled from the garage that Leno made the decision to not restore the car. "I'm going to keep it just the way it is," he said.

The car has already been displayed on the lawn at the Pebble Beach Concours and was featured in a Discovery Channel special.

1931 Duesenberg Model J

Leno had heard the rumors about a Model J Duesenberg—the most prestigious model in the company's line—for at least ten years. The stories revolved around a tale that in the early 1930s, the original owner of a Duesenberg parked it in a garage in New York City and never came back to pick it up. But according to Leno, stories of Duesenbergs are many, and almost none are true.

"There are some vehicles—Vincent Motorcycles, Alfa Romeos, some Harley-Davidsons—that have myths that develop around them," Leno said. "Duesies are certainly that type of vehicle."

Leno was not able to resist the appeal of the myth. While he and his wife were in New York City for a shopping trip several years ago, he decided to take a side trip and do a little hunting.

"I'm not much of a shopper, so I decided to hit public garages and see if I could actually find some of these lost New York City collector cars that I'd always heard about," he said. "I'd go up to a garage operator and ask if there were any old cars in there, and they'd say 'Sure.' And sometimes you'd find a 1920s Rolls-Royce, and sometimes you'd find a Ford Maverick.

"Eventually, I walked into a garage on West Fifty-Seventh Street off Park Avenue, and the guy said to go upstairs and take a look. There, on the third floor, next to the window, was the Duesenberg I'd heard about."

The myth was true.

"It was the last unrestored, original owner Duesenberg on Earth," Ema said. "It was a 1931, was parked in the garage in 1933, and not removed for seventy years. It only had seven thousand eighty-five miles on the odometer. The original upholstery would have been in great shape, but someone piled a bunch of old tires in the car about fifty years ago, so the chemicals in the rubber stained and ruined the interior."

The car had a Woods Body mounted to the Duesenberg chassis.

Woods, according to Leno, was the body company that built President Abraham Lincoln's funeral coach.

The car was parked next to a window that was always open. According to Ema, there was six inches of dirt all around the car because nobody had swept around it in almost three-quarters of a century. And because there was a small leak above the car, when it rained, over seventy years—drip, drip, drip—a hole developed in the fender.

"Other people had known about this car," Leno said. "I had heard about the hidden New York Duesenberg for years, but when I actually found it, I didn't want to lose it. So I made up a story—no, it was an absolute lie—that the car couldn't be removed from its third-floor home because the new elevator that had been installed several years earlier was too small to fit the car."

Leno contacted the Duesie's owner, and he heard those words so many of us barn finders hate to hear: "No, it's not for sale."

But then he heard from a friend that it might, in fact, be for sale, but the matter was complicated.

Since the car had sat for so long, and the original owner's son was behind on paying for the storage, there was about $80,000 owed in parking fees. So when most of the people who had known about the car offered $10,000, the owner simply said no.

"The highest offers he received were about thirty-five thousand to forty-five thousand dollars, but it was worth more than one hundred thousand dollars," Leno said. "So when I offered the owner fair market value, he jumped at it. I think I got it for a good price, and I didn't treat these people like idiots."

The Duesenberg was trucked from New York to California, where it was delivered first to Ema's shop, where it was inventoried and cleaned up. Then it was delivered to Leno's Big Dog Garage.

According to Leno, this car will be sympathetically restored.

"It's just a little too far gone to be preserved," he said.

Once the Model J was removed from its "Manhattan tomb" and inspected, Leno decided the car needed to be restored from the ground up. He is now in the middle of that restoration in the Burbank facility known as Big Dog Garage. *Randy Ema*

Leno isn't finished with searching for forgotten cars. He's on the hunt for a couple of intriguing cars he recently heard about.

"There's a 1933 Cadillac that was apparently put on blocks and properly stored in 1935," he said. "It's still owned by the woman who bought it new. She's ninety-five years old."

And he has learned that the same gentleman who bought the Duesenberg Model J also bought a Bugatti in 1936 or 1937. And it, too, is hidden somewhere in New York City. But Jay's not speaking.

"I think lots of old stuff that was found in the 1960s is going to come back on the market," he said.

And Leno is going to try to own as many of those old relics as he can.

THE ENTERPRISING PRIEST AND HIS BUBBLE-SCREENED BOONDOGGLE

Anthony Alfred Juliano prayed he was making the right decision. The young man from Philadelphia was an enthusiast of cars and airplanes and had a knack for drawing.

In 1938, someone at General Motors was shown Juliano's car sketches. They were impressed enough with the eighteen-year-old lad's work to offer him enrollment in Harley Earl's newly opened school for automotive design students. GM's offer came just too late; Juliano had just decided to enter the priesthood.

Torn between two loves, Juliano was committed to becoming a man of the cloth. Father Juliano attended the Holy Ghost seminary in Philadelphia from 1934 to 1940. He became an ordained priest in 1946, one year before graduating from Ferndale in Connecticut with dual degrees: a Bachelor of Arts and a degree in divinity. He joined the order of the Holy Ghost Fathers and began teaching at the Virginia Military Academy. Later, he became an art professor at Duquesne University in Pittsburgh.

In an attempt to get his doctorate in art and aerodynamics from Yale, Juliano was transferred to St. Mary's in Branford, Connecticut, where he was assistant pastor.

Even as Father Juliano was reading the Bible and preparing for his doctorate, he was also reading technical manuals, *Mechanix Illustrated*, and every car magazine he could get his hands on.

As he pored over magazines and manuals, he thought about how to create the safest car on the road.

"He wanted to build the safest car in the world for his parishioners," said Andy Saunders, an auto restorer and custom car builder from Poole, England, and an authority on Father Juliano. Saunders owns the Juliano-built Aurora seen on these pages.

"His thinking was so far ahead of his time. He was a genius."

As opposed to today, where Volvo and Mercedes advertisements shout their companies' crash-test results as a marketing strategy, it was Juliano's belief that people cared more about style than safety.

Americans "won't pay for safety," he was quoted as saying in a 1955 interview with Connecticut's *New Haven Register*. He sought to build a car that combined "unity and originality of design" that would have consumers flocking to buy his car for its beauty and acquiring the safety benefits as a bonus.

As can be seen from the accompanying photos of the Aurora, beauty is indeed in the eye of the beholder. Nonetheless, Father Juliano surged forward with his plans.

Selling the idea of car design to his superiors on the basis that it aided his thesis studies, he set up shop in an old horse stable in Branford and bought

Father Anthony Alfred Juliano created quite a stir as he drove the Aurora to its press introduction at the Hotel New Yorker on Thirty-Fifth Street in 1957. The trip from Connecticut was plagued with mechanical breakdowns, and the ninety-minute drive took nearly eleven hours. *Associated Press*

a wrecked 1953 Buick Roadmaster. He stripped the Buick's sheet metal, straightened the mangled frame, and spent the next four years designing and tinkering on what he hoped would be the safest, most beautiful car ever built. The Aurora was named for his young niece, Dawn; *aurora* is Latin for "dawn."

"Uncle Al was a part of our household during every holiday," said Father Juliano's niece Dawn O'Mara. "I can tell you that he definitely was not a hot rodder. He didn't know anything about the mechanical parts of cars. He was more of an artist and loved to paint in oil."

He began by building a clay scale model of his design, then used plywood and fiberglass to construct a body mold. According to O'Mara, her uncle worked with Owens/Corning in the development of the Aurora's body. The roof and gullwing-type window canopy was constructed of shatterproof resin.

Father Juliano worked tirelessly on the car, aided by sympathetic parishioners and a team of teenage boys eager to get their hands dirty working on cars.

Despite the Aurora's ungainly appearance, Father Juliano designed safety features into his car that were decades ahead of the automotive industry. Starting with the passenger compartment, one of the most obvious features is the car's bubble windshield. Father Juliano specified it be made of shatterproof resin so that it would be difficult for passengers to hit their heads on the windshield, a common injury at the time. Seat belts were also built into the car's design.

He mounted the car's four "captain's chairs" high and toward the center of the car in order to give better protection in the event of a side impact. The four seats were also pedestal-mounted, allowing occupants to rotate up to 360 degrees prior to a crash for better protection.

The Aurora interior also featured a race car–type roll cage made of stainless steel, recessed gauges, and eight inches of padding on the dashboard. The car featured a collapsible steering column and side-impact protection bars. The Aurora's exterior featured a front end with a huge foam-filled crush-zone that doubled as a "cowcatcher" to cradle errant pedestrians. The spare tire was located under the nose to assist in crash protection. Above the crush zone were six headlights, which were to be replaced with a light bar if the car were put into production.

The bubble windshield eliminated the need for windshield wipers, because like a jet plane, the car's speed would push rainwater to the sides. The Aurora also featured an automatic jacking system to aid in flat-tire repair or other servicing.

Father Juliano wrote a sales brochure that claimed the Aurora was the world's safest car. The brochure noted that the car could be ordered with any type of powerplant: Cadillac, Lincoln, Imperial, Packard, Bugatti, or Mercedes-Benz. It also listed as options such items as fuel injection and supercharging, as well as a wide assortment of interior and exterior finishes.

The Custom Automobile Corporation of America, Father Juliano's enterprise, claimed that the Aurora's fiberglass styling was "the most advanced in the world for a production automobile. It is built to last many years and will remain substantially the same year-in and year-out—a lifetime masterpiece of automotive engineering and design."

The promise was never fulfilled, however. The prototype cost $30,000 to construct, even though Father Juliano said he could manufacture models for $12,000 each and make a profit. But in 1957, the price was huge; even though it didn't include all the innovative safety features of the Aurora, a new Cadillac during the same period was less than $5,000.

The unfinished car was displayed at the 1956 Hartford (Connecticut) Autorama and was featured in the event program centerfold.

In 1957, en route to a press function to introduce the car to the New York media, it broke down at least fifteen times on Father Juliano and needed to be towed to seven different service stations for repairs to unclog the fuel line. Apparently, the Buick on which the Aurora was based had sat idle for all the years of design and construction, causing the gas tank to rust and clog the lines.

The trip from Branford, Connecticut, to Manhattan—which should have taken ninety minutes—took nearly eleven hours. At 3 p.m., Father Juliano once again called, saying that he was getting the Aurora's battery recharged in Harlem.

The media that had assembled at the Hotel New Yorker for the 8 a.m. press conference started to dissipate, and by the time the Aurora rolled up at 4 p.m., few media crews remained. The Associated Press, *New York Times*, and *Bridgeport Post* covered the car's arrival, but the media neglected to cover the car's safety features and instead mocked its voyage from Connecticut.

"Dream Car Arrives from Connecticut After Nightmare of Breakdowns," read the *Times* headline. The *Bridgeport Post* wrote, "Auto Built by Priest for Safety Perils Traffic," referring to the police request that Father Juliano move his car because of the rubbernecking traffic jam it had caused on Thirty-Fifth Street.

The Aurora's New York debut was supposed to kick off a 120-city tour around the United States, where Father Juliano had hoped to take orders from customers. Unfortunately, the Aurora's styling didn't excite the public the way Father Juliano had hoped.

Father Juliano's project failed to attract investors or customers, so the car sat forlorn behind a Connecticut body shop for decades before being rescued by British car customizer Andy Saunders after he saw it in a magazine. *Vince Leto*

Additionally, questions began to arise about the funding for Father Juliano's automotive project. The car's development was at least partially funded by parishioners of St. Mary's church, and his superiors accused him of misappropriation of church donations. Others accused Father Juliano of spending parishioner donations not only for the Aurora project but also for himself. Church officials met with Father Juliano, and he was summarily disciplined.

Father Juliano's niece, Dawn O'Mara, has her own opinion regarding the issue of her uncle's financial worries. "There were a lot of local folks who were impressed with Uncle Al's innovative ideas on safety features," O'Mara said. "You know, the seat belts, the windshield; they all wanted to get on the bandwagon because of all the positive hype.

"There was the intention of great profits."

O'Mara feels that many of the parishioners who invested their savings into the Custom Automotive Corporation's Aurora project began to have second thoughts once the shine started to wear off Father Juliano's dream. They sought their money returned or at least a way to save face.

Others suggest that General Motors was behind the accusations. These theories claim that the Aurora's safety features were so advanced that it threatened GM's own safety programs and the huge corporation's reputation. GM denied any involvement.

Regardless of blame, Father Juliano was drummed out of the Order of the Holy Ghost. He was investigated by the FBI and the Internal Revenue Service, but the investigations led nowhere. Father Juliano compared himself to the late Preston Tucker, a manufacturer of the Torpedo, which was so advanced that he claims he was forced out of business in 1948 by the big Detroit automakers who didn't want to disturb the industry's status quo. Tucker also was accused of financial scandal, which was proved to be unfounded.

What wasn't publicized, though, was that Father Juliano had also put himself into deep personal debt financing the project to completion. He was bankrupt, and the Aurora was given as collateral to a repair shop for unpaid repair bills. The car went through several hands before landing in a field behind McPhee's Body Shop in Cheshire, Connecticut.

Juliano went on to live in Florida before moving back to Philadelphia, where he became involved in art restoration.

According to his niece, Father Juliano worked with Sotheby's and other art auction houses on painting and gold-leaf frame restoration. "He was an artist in his own right," O'Mara said. "My brothers and I still own some of Uncle Al's paintings, and they are very, very good."

O'Mara said that her uncle also planned to build another car and had sketches and plans for a new design, but he never went further than the planning stages.

In 1989, her uncle was doing art research in the Philadelphia Public Library when he suffered a massive heart attack. He was rushed to nearby Hahnemann Hospital, where he was put on life support and fell into a coma.

"The hospital didn't know who he was, because his car keys were in his pocket and his wallet was in his car in the library parking lot," she said.

"My brother and I were called to identify him. Then, because my own father [Anthony Raymond Juliano] was in such bad condition, also in the hospital, my brother and I were asked to sign to take Uncle Al off life support." He died on March 2, 1989, and he was buried in the Catholic cemetery in the Drexel Hill section of Philadelphia.

By the time Father Juliano was laid to rest, his Aurora safety car had already been resting in the field for more than thirty years. The body shop owner attempted to sell the car for $10,000 in 1978, but there were no interested parties. An issue of the British magazine *Thoroughbred & Classic Cars* featured the Aurora in their "Discovered" section, which highlights interesting classic cars that are found by readers. The car caught the attention of one interested reader—Andy Saunders. "I'd seen that car before in an old schoolbook," he said.

Saunders showed the picture to his father, who said, "That's the ugliest car I've ever seen."

Saunders, who runs a custom auto fabrication shop called Andy Saunders Kustoms, Kampers and Kars in Poole, England, has always dreamed of owning a prototype dream car. He felt this was his chance.

"I studied the picture in the magazine and saw the name of the body shop in the background and was able to read the phone number," he said.

Saunders called the owner of the shop where the Aurora had now rested for at least thirty-four years.

"I paid one thousand five hundred dollars for it without ever seeing it in person," he said. "When it arrived in England, it was absolutely knocked. It was scrap. It was falling to pieces.

"All the door frames—the A-pillars, the B-pillars, firewall, wheel arches—they were all made of wood. Having sat in the field for so long, the water completely delaminated the wood."

But the fiberglass body was a different story. The wood would need to be fabricated and fitted piece-by-piece, meaning a tough manual labor chore for Saunders. The fiberglass had deteriorated so badly it was almost melted, according to Saunders.

"Father Juliano was so far ahead of his time, he was considered weird. But I'm convinced he was a genius. The driver sits at least four-and-a-half feet from the windshield; there had never been a car built like that."

When Saunders realized what he had bought, he became depressed. He dove in and spent virtually every night and weekend restoring, in some ways remanufacturing, the Aurora. He was able to retain the original chassis and running gear, front and rear fenders, and hood.

"Custom cars are a hobby for me," he said. "It's nothing for me to spend eighteen or nineteen hours a day working on cars. I can work eight a.m. to five p.m. working on cars in my business, then work until two a.m. working on my own cars. I think they are the most exciting vehicles in the world.

"The roof structure held the whole [body] together, so we had to cut it in half to disassemble and reassemble the body," said Saunders, "or else the car would have fallen apart."

The largest challenge Saunders has faced is in replicating the unusual windshield.

"I can't get anyone to build a windshield like he [Father Juliano] did," he said. "The one we built turned yellow in five years, yet the original sat outside for more than thirty years and still was clear but unfortunately unusable."

Saunders has copies of the original sales brochure from when the Aurora was displayed at the Hotel New Yorker in 1957, and every magazine the car was featured in, but unfortunately all the photos are in black and white. One cover photo, though, in *Motor Trend*, showed the car in black and silver, so that's how the car is finished.

"The picture looked to be 'color washed,' so I'm not quite sure of the exact colors of the Aurora," he said. "But I had nothing else to go with and couldn't find a single chip of original paint on the car."

So far Saunders has spent $12,000 working with aircraft manufacturers trying to copy that windshield.

"That car owes me," he said. "It's the most expensive car I've ever restored. The car cost me seventy-five to eighty thousand dollars, exclusive of the hours I've invested."

So far, Saunder's restored Aurora has been featured in a number of magazines and the prestigious Goodwood Festival of Speed in England. The Petersen Automotive Museum in Los Angeles also has granted a standing invitation for the car if it ever comes to the United States.

Saunders, though, doesn't pull any punches regarding his feelings for the finished product.

"I hate the bloody thing," he said. "I wish I'd never bought it.

"At least if I could register the bloody thing and drive it on the road, it would be different. But this bloody windshield!"

THE GREEN HORNET STRIKES AGAIN

How many youths have fallen in love with a car that starred in their favorite television show or movie? I've met folks who have had lifelong passions for the *Batmobile*, the *Monkeemobile*, and the green Mustang fastback from the movie *Bullitt*.

Karl Kirchner can't explain why he fell in love with the *Black Beauty* from the *Green Hornet* television series.

"Even as a kid, I just really liked that particular car," said Kirchner, forty-six, from Spartanburg, South Carolina. "I was just a little kid, three or four years old, but I liked the show more than *Batman*, because it was more serious.

"I even had a Corgi toy of the car."

A lifelong quest ensued for Kirchner as he sought information on the innovative television show car.

I know a thing or two about the *Black Beauty* as well. The car was built by late customizer Dean Jeffries, who claimed it as one of the favorite cars he had built in his long career. I wrote the book *Dean Jeffries: 50 Fabulous Years in Hot Rods, Racing & Film* (MBI Publishing Company, 2009), which chronicles this fascinating man's career.

The *Black Beauty* started life as a 1966 Chrysler Imperial and provided transport for the crime-fighting duo of the Green Hornet (played by Van Williams) and his faithful sidekick, Kato (played by Bruce Lee).

The Imperial was radically modified with crime-fighting equipment, including a front grille-mounted cannon and a pair of rocket launchers below each headlight. The rear of the car featured bumpers that flipped open to reveal rockets and

This is how *Green Hornet* enthusiast Karl Kirchner discovered his dream car, the *Black Beauty*. The Dean Jeffries design was crammed into a tight Michigan garage. Kirchner made friends with the elderly female owner. When she passed away, her heirs thought that he would be the ideal next owner. *Karl Kirchner*

flamethrowers. Behind the rear wheels were two small brushes that would sweep away tire tracks on dirt roads.

But even though the *Black Beauty* featured dozens of radical—albeit fictional—options, most viewers never truly connected with the car the way fans of the *Batman* series connected with the *Batmobile*.

"They messed it up," said Jeffries when I interviewed him for his biography. "They made me paint the car black, and they only used it for night shots. You couldn't see it!"

So even though Jeffries invested blood, sweat, and tears building the two *Black Beauties*, the car went unappreciated among most viewers.

Except Karl Kirchner.

The show was cancelled after only one season, and the studio offered Jeffries the pair of cars for $1,500. When he turned down the offer, the cars fell into obscurity. The number 1 car, which was used for most of the television production, was restored and eventually sold to the Petersen Automotive Museum in Los Angeles.

"The first car resurfaced in 1991, and everyone thought it was the only car that was built," Kirchner said. "It had been privately owned and [Dean Jeffries] restored the car for the owner."

But Kirchner knew a second *Black Beauty* existed. The second car was used occasionally for the television program but mostly for promotional displays and car shows.

Kirchner called Dean sometime in the late 1980s and asked him if he knew where the second *Black Beauty* might be. He responded, "No, but if I did, I would have bought it already."

"He kept pretty good track of his cars over the years," Kirchner said. "It bothered him that he didn't know where the other car was."

The second car was sold originally to *Green Hornet* producer William Dozier, who kept it until 1969. Fellow customizer George Barris negotiated with Dozier to sell the car to Jack Button, a collector who intended to build an auto museum at Disneyland. But the museum project fizzled, and in 1971, *Black Beauty* number 2 was sold to a Mr. J. J. Born, but only after the car was "modified" by George Barris with new paint, pinstriping, and new wheels. In 1984, the car was sold for $10,000 to Constantine Tatooles, a cardio surgeon.

Eventually, *Black Beauty* was sold at a Kruse auction in Auburn, Indiana, to a seventy-eight-year-old woman, Opal Wall.

Kirchner (pictured) purchased the car in 2001 and began a thorough restoration. This is how the car appears today. *Karl Kirchner*

"Wall was single and a certified car nut," Kirchner said. "She also owned a black 1955 Ford Thunderbird, which she bought new, and a black 1969 Lincoln Mark III. She loved black cars.

"She bought it at the auction because she liked its looks and thought it looked similar to a presidential car. She displayed the car for two years in the Gilmore Museum in Kalamazoo, Michigan, then put [it] into storage a couple of blocks from her home."

Kirchner still hadn't located the car but, through a stroke of luck, was given a couple of clues by the then-owner of *Black Beauty* number 1.

"Louis Ringe found paperwork on car number two in the glove box of car number one," said Kirchner. "When he found out I was interested in it, he gave me the VIN. This was probably in 1999.

"Within twenty-four hours, I found out that a woman, who turned out to be Opal Wall, owned the car."

Kirchner called Wall's home, but there was no answer. He learned that he had to call earlier in the day, when Opal was in the part of her house where she could hear the phone.

Eventually, they developed a telephone friendship because they both loved to talk about cars.

"Have you ever thought about selling the *Black Beauty*?" Kirchner asked Wall.

"Yes, people need to see this car," she answered. "Why don't you come up here to see it?"

So at the next opportunity, Kirchner drove from his South Carolina home to southern Michigan to see the car of his boyhood dreams.

Wall was apparently eagerly awaiting his arrival; as soon as Kirchner pulled in the driveway, she bolted out the front door and jumped into his car. She explained that the car was stored at a nearby garage owned by a heating and air conditioning business. When they got to the garage, just a few blocks away, they met the grumpy garage owner.

"He never took his eyes off of me," Kirchner said. "I walked around and looked at the car as best I could, because it was sandwiched between old Chevys.

"I looked under the hood and could barely squeeze between the cars to check the car's VIN. And it only had eleven thousand miles on the odometer. Once I saw that, I knew it was Jeffries's car."

Wall said he could take pictures of the car, but the grumpy garage owner jumped in and said no. But Wall gave Kirchner a Polaroid photo of the car.

"We drove back to her house and sat around talking price," he said. "She was receptive. But I wanted to give her time to talk it over with her family. So I drove home thinking all the way about owning that car."

He waited a few days, then called Wall. No answer. He called over and over for more than a month until one day a man answered. The man turned out to be Wall's nephew, and he told Kirchner that his aunt had a stroke and had fallen.

She was in the hospital.

Kirchner sent flowers to her, which she appreciated, but less than thirty days later, she died. This was in June 2000.

"I kept track of obituary notices online," he said. "I found out through the courts that Wall's niece had been appointed executor of the estate. I told her I had been speaking to her aunt about purchasing the car. She said she wanted to talk to the man who owned car number one, as well as to George Barris."

In June 2001, a purchase was negotiated for the same amount that Kirchner and Wall had discussed a couple of years earlier.

When the paperwork was signed, Kirchner had the car shipped to South Carolina.

"Once home, I looked at it for a couple of years," he said. "It was beginning to show its age. It had cracked paint and the leather seat top was torn where Barris had customized it by gluing flashlights to it.

"After a few years of just looking at it, I decided to dive in and do a complete restoration. My first intention was to completely strip the car and rebuild it like Jeffries did, but then I realized if I did that, it would erase the fingerprints of Dean Jeffries."

A partial restoration complicated Kirchner's task, because instead of just purchasing and installing a hot rod wiring kit, he repaired the old, complicated wiring harness that Jeffries had constructed decades earlier. Most of the electric motors that actuated various special effects on the car were military issued, so Kirchner had a difficult time sourcing replacement units.

"I've done probably a dozen restorations in my life, and by far, this is the most difficult and expensive car I've done," Kirchner said. "First of all, it's an Imperial, and most of them probably wound up in demolition derbies. It's not a 'Cuda or a Road Runner, so people don't save parts, so finding them was a challenge.

"It has taken three to four years to restore the car, which is interesting, because Dean built the original car in just two to three weeks."

OTHERWORLDLY
ORBITRON

It was hard to escape Ed "Big Daddy" Roth when I was a kid. To young guys in the 1960s, Roth's google-eyed character, Rat Fink, was plastered on T-shirts, and his monster cars were all the rage for kids of a certain model-kit-building age.

Roth, an artist, cartoonist, pinstriper, and custom car designer and builder was all the rage in the sixties, and much of model kit manufacturer Revell's revenues was based on scale versions of Roth's creations. The man was a brand and industry onto himself, having created the weirdo T-shirt craze that others quickly copied. Some of Roth's more memorable automotive creations some readers may remember include *Tweedy Pie*, *Mysterion*, *Beatnik Bandit*, *Surfite*, *Outlaw*, and the *Road Agent*.

As a kid, Beau Boeckmann was also a Roth freak. Now, Boeckmann has taken his interest to another level—he has established a small museum dedicated to Roth vehicles and memorabilia.

Boeckmann is vice president of Galpin Motors, a Ford dealership in Los Angeles that his father bought in 1946. So he has literally grown up in the car business. And when the news spread that Roth's *Orbitron* had been spotted in Mexico after going unseen for decades, Boeckmann was all over it.

It was found by El Paso, Texas–based car hunter Michael Lightbourn. Lightbourn frequently travels south of the border in search of significant American cars that migrated to Mexico and stumbled on *Orbitron* in the city of Juarez, where it was basically a dumpster in front of a sex and video shop. The shop's owner was reluctant to sell, but the partly destroyed hot rod had languished

After being used as a makeshift dumpster in Mexico, the Ed "Big Daddy" Roth *Orbitron* was purchased and brought back to California for a full restoration by Beau Boeckmann. *Beau Boeckmann Collection*

in front of that store for years, and Lightbourn convinced the owner to sell. *Orbitron* had deteriorated badly over the decades; the unique front-nose cone that carried the car's distinguished three-headlight pod was missing, and what remained elsewhere was in poor condition. "Michael [Lightbourn] and I started talking at the 2007 SEMA Show," Boeckmann said. Lightbourn wanted to keep the car and restore it. "But when I told him my vision for the car, we made a deal. So I got on a plane and flew to El Paso to see the car."

Boeckmann saw the car in all its depressing glory. He and Lightbourn then drove to Juarez to see where the car had been parked for all those years. "I was a little bit nervous, because Juarez is known as the most dangerous city in North America," he said.

Once Boeckmann had the car back in LA, he worked with many of the car's original contractors to assist in the *Orbitron's* restoration. Larry Watson and Bill Carter painted the car when it was new in 1964; they painted the car again during its restoration. Joe Perez originally stitched the *Orbitron's* upholstery and was hired by Boeckmann the second time around.

"The toughest part of the restoration was finding the original type TV set that sat in the dashboard," Boeckmann said. "Roth did everything by eye," he added; nothing was measured.

"We didn't change any of Roth's techniques during the restoration." So if it's still a little out-of-this-world, well, all the better.

185

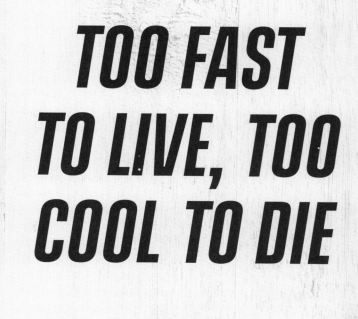

TOO FAST
TO LIVE, TOO
COOL TO DIE

A PROPANE GAS DELIVERY MAN'S DISCOVERY

Electric company meter-readers, landscapers, and other deliverymen possibly have the best opportunity to discover vehicles "just out of view" from car collectors. After all, they can venture onto properties, look behind bushes, and peer into barns. The story of Cobra CSX2149 begins this way, when a propane gas delivery driver looked into a customer's remote barn near Indianapolis, Indiana, in 1993.

What the deliveryman saw was a small sports car he believed was a Triumph or an MG. He mentioned the discovery to a friend, who mentioned it to a friend, who then told his young cousin. We'll call this cousin Johnny.

Well, being an enterprising youth, Johnny knocked on the owner's door and asked if he could please see the sports car. Opening the barn doors and climbing behind tractors, cultivators, and other farm equipment, Johnny came across an incredible discovery: an authentic A.C. Cobra.

Turns out that the owner, Dr. Bryan Molloy, was a chemist with Lilly Pharmaceuticals and helped develop Prozac. According to his widow, he purchased the Cobra in 1968 or 1969 from an ad in an Indianapolis newspaper. It was already painted brown (over the original white), and he drove it for a couple of years. But his wife eventually convinced him that it was too unsafe to drive, and he parked it in a friend's garage when he lived in the city. When the couple purchased the farm outside of Indianapolis, they moved it to an unheated barn.

Cobra CSX2149, the 149th Cobra produced, was stored in an Indiana barn for nearly thirty years. The raccoon living in it was angry about his eviction, but he had been a bad tenant, having eaten much of the original leather interior and carpet. *Jim Maxwell*

The Shelby American World Registry lists CSX2149 as the 149th 289 Cobra manufactured, and it was shipped to Shelby American in July 1963. CSX2149 was manufactured in off-white with a red leather interior and was ordered with Class A accessories, including a luggage rack and whitewall tires, for a total price of $5,415.50. The car was then shipped to Ford's district office in Davenport, Iowa, for promotional use. Not much more is known of the car until it was purchased by Molloy.

Johnny asked the widow if the car was for sale. He was told that yes it was, but in restored condition, it would be worth $80,000 to $90,000. Yet when Johnny offered $30,000, the widow said, "Son, you've bought yourself a car!" Not a bad return on a one-time $4,000 investment. The problem was that Johnny didn't have the money, and he was denied a bank loan, so he borrowed $30,000 from suspicious relatives. He promised to pay them back when he sold the Cobra.

After unloading the accumulated piles of junk that had buried the car for decades and dragging it out of the barn with a tractor, Johnny discovered that it had been the home of a thirty-pound raccoon who didn't take very kindly to being displaced once the tonneau cover was removed. It seems that Mr. Raccoon had eaten much of the red leather covering the seats and most of the carpet, but the car was generally in good condition.

The car had been driven only twenty-one thousand miles and still retained much of its original equipment, including its low-rise cast-iron intake manifold, the small Y-type exhaust headers, and sparkplug wires. It sported a cheap, metallic bronze paint job over the original off-white.

Johnny brought the car home, and word spread quickly that a long-missing Cobra had been discovered. Bids began to come in fast and furiously from various collectors in the United States and even Canada. Even though the highest bid reached $85,000 (from a Canadian collector), the car was sold to local collector David Doll of Indianapolis for $60,000.

The Hi-Po 289 engine had not run in twenty-five years, but with a new battery and a splash of fuel, the car was running within fifteen minutes. Doll later installed new Koni shocks and refurbished the car mechanically but left the exterior and the cosmetics as found.

Doll had a friend who owned a muscle car museum in Gatlinburg, Tennessee, and he put the Cobra on display there for a while before selling it to Greenville, South Carolina, Harley-Davidson dealer Billy Weaver—who then sold it to Greensboro, North Carolina, Cobra enthusiast Jim Maxwell and buying partner Tom Cotter (yes, that Tom Cotter).

Maxwell and Cotter disassembled the car, had it repainted white, and reupholstered the red interior to repair the raccoon's damage. Instead of restoring the car, they refurbished it and refreshed as many of the removable parts as possible. After spending many years as an ugly duckling, CSX2149 was transformed once again into a beautiful swan.

The Shelby American Automobile Club (SAAC) says that very few original Cobras are not accounted for, but one wonders how many still reside in barns just beyond view. Fate played a hand in Johnny's find, as within thirty days of his purchase, the barn that had housed CSX2149 for so many years burned to the ground.

THE AUTOMOTIVE ARCHAEOLOGIST

Most auto enthusiasts would feel it quite an accomplishment to uncover two or three barn-find Porsches in their lifetime. But Steve Demosthenes, who sees himself as an "automotive archaeologist," has spent the better part of forty years pursuing and purchasing 356 series Porsches from hidden places all over the United States. He has uncovered more than a hundred of the German sports cars, and even though the supply is drying up, he occasionally still discovers another one in a barn or behind a fence.

His fascination with cars started early—not a surprise considering he grew up in the shadow of the Indianapolis 500 in the 1960s. "My first car was a souped-up '36 Ford sedan, followed by a '31 Ford with a Chevy engine, a '55 Chevy, a split-window '63 Corvette, and a three hundred ninety-six–cubic-inch Sting Ray roadster," Demosthenes said. "All that power was intoxicating, but once I got a ride in my boss' sports car—a '58 Porsche Speedster, at age sixteen—it left an impression that never faded.

"I remember it to this day: it was white, and it was the only Porsche I've ever seen with Daytona knock-off wire wheels."

Just a few years later, Demosthenes got his own sports car, an Austin-Healey "Bugeye" Sprite, but in 1968 he decided to buy a more practical sports car, so he narrowed his choices down to an Alfa Romeo and a Porsche 356.

"They were both in my price range, so don't ask me why, but I bought the Porsche. I eventually sold that Porsche and bought another and another, never with the intention of making a profit, but just for the opportunity to drive a variety of cars," he said.

By 1970, he was living in Los Angeles and had hooked up with a fellow Porsche fan from Baltimore. "He had a little bit of money, so I convinced him that we should fly to the Midwest, buy Porsches, and then drive them back to California to sell," Demosthenes said, adding that while Porsches weren't in demand in the Midwest, a willing buyer could always be found on the West Coast.

These were the days prior to the Internet, so Demosthenes relied heavily on the *Auto Trader* newspaper to find the cars. "I placed hundreds of want ads with a photo of an old Porsche to grab attention. When the *Auto Trader* went national, I hit the mother lode." One of his best discoveries came after Demosthenes got a call from a guy in Brunswick, Georgia, responding to an *Auto Trader* ad. The caller mentioned that his recently deceased father had been a Porsche restorer and now those cars and parts needed to be sold.

"I told him I was interested and drove up to see what he had," Demosthenes said. "Way back in the woods and down this country road, there was a strange-looking concrete structure with some totally rusted-out body shells and a wonderfully original silver 1954 Continental Cabriolet. I immediately bought the car and had it trucked away to a friend's shop in Jacksonville, Florida." But the seller was very evasive about the possibility of the others being available for purchase.

One of Steve Demosthenes's barn finds in 1970. Inspecting the car is one of his favorite traveling companions, a Great Dane named Tara. Demosthenes spent several years traveling the United States buying Porsche 356s, driving them to California, and selling them. *Steve Demosthenes*

Another one of the cars Demosthenes attempted to buy from a man who was actually a drug dealer. Demosthenes thought he was purchasing six or seven 356 Porsches, but instead he and his girlfriend were temporarily arrested and questioned, then released. He had to return the cars and lost $5,000. *Steve Demosthenes*

Weeks later, after many phone calls, Demosthenes coerced the seller into showing him the other cars and parts, and that visit uncovered six or seven Porsches and tons of new old stock parts. Another deal was struck, and Demosthenes began hauling the cars out. "On my last trip with the trailer, as we were loading parts, my girlfriend and I walked out of the garage to face several federal agents with their guns drawn," Demosthenes said with a laugh. "Turns out the cars didn't belong to his father–but instead to his drug-dealing ex-partner who was wanted for murder and was on the run.

"So I had to return the Continental Cabriolet and all the other cars. I don't know what ever happened to the cars. I wound up losing about five thousand dollars on the deal. But losing that '54 Cabriolet was a heartbreaker."

Another barn-find story sparked by a 1991 *Auto Trader* want ad revolves around a 356 a guy knew about in eastern Washington state. "He told me about another 'old guy,' Paul, who had a three fifty-six sitting behind his garage," Demosthenes said. "So we drove to the location and met the owner. He showed us a very rusty, ratty 'A' coupe that was sitting outside."

In those days, cars like this were only considered parts cars, so Demosthenes wasn't very interested in it. Then the "old guy" told him he had another Porsche in the garage.

Carefully navigating the yard littered with old lawn mowers, a crashed airplane, and assorted Porsche parts, they got to the garage, where Demosthenes could see a roof profile of a coupe from under boxes and years of discarded junk. Upon closer investigation, he found that the car's rear clip had been cut off, and it had a considerable number of inner body panels that needed repair. It also had some holes cut out of the driver's side rear inner fender well, which he asked the owner about.

"Oh, all the Carreras had those for the oil cooler," the owner said. Of course, the mention of the word *Carrera* made Demosthenes's heart rate almost double. "But I fought to show no interest or enthusiasm," he said. "I continued to keep the conversation flowing, still not fully convinced. I asked him where the engine was. He said, 'Oh, it's in the house.' He then showed me the cowl that covers the generator: it was unmistakably Carrera.

"But would he sell? NO!"

For the next thirteen years, Demosthenes continued to contact Paul about the car—even making the 150-mile drive to visit—but the answer was always no. But finally, in 2004, Demosthenes convinced the owner to sell the Carrera four-cam engine in exchange for a freshly rebuilt 356 engine, which he loaded into his truck and drove to Paul's.

"After thirteen years, I finally saw the four-cam engine hanging from a hoist in his guest bedroom, surrounded by old newspapers and trash; it had been

This is Porsche No. 5047, which was built in August 1950. It was the thirty-eighth Porsche 356 built and is the oldest known coupe built in Stuttgart. *Steve Demosthenes*

This photo of a coupe and a roadster was taken in the mid-1980s in a Gulfport, Mississippi, backyard. The owner wouldn't sell. Demosthenes believes that several hurricanes have most likely hit the area by now, and the cars—if still there—are likely totaled. *Steve Demosthenes*

placed there in 1969. The Carrera engine was finally mine," Demosthenes said. "I went back to see him and inquire about the rest of the Carrera, a 1956 sunroof model, originally aquamarine metallic.

"But what I had feared all these years finally happened: Paul died three weeks after I purchased the engine. He was sitting alone in his chair and was discovered by neighbors six days later. I contacted his brother, and I was finally able to acquire the Carrera body [in 2005]. This might be my last great barn find, but what a find it was!"

His final memorable Porsche-find tale starts while Demosthenes was traveling from Hood River, Oregon, back to the Florida Keys in his 1962 Notchback S90. Along the way, he hunted for old Porsches.

"While in Dallas, Texas, I was asking some local Porsche guys if they knew of any older Porsches for sale. I was told there was this weird, old professor in Denton, Texas, who had an ancient Porsche," he said. "The Pre-As [the very earliest] Porsches were not the 'hot topic' in those days. I drove up to see the car, and there it was, parked alongside the house. It was very, very rusty with years of moss, dirt, and leaves included. No one was home, so I took some photos and left a note."

Then, after Demosthenes returned to Key West, he got a call from the professor, who explained that he had bought the Porsche in Germany in the early 1970s. Years later, he shipped it to the United States, Alabama to be exact, and then the car made the move with him to Texas. However, its time in Texas was pretty much spent sitting outside the garage, rusting.

Demosthenes first offer of $4,000 for the relic was happily accepted, and it wasn't until later that he discovered the uniqueness of his purchase. "The factory sent me the Kardex [or record sheet] for number 5047, which confirmed it was built in August 1950 while Professor Ferdinand Porsche was still alive," Demosthenes says. "I tried to sell it in the States, but there were no takers. So I had a trip planned to Europe to visit as many Porsche guys as I could, from Sweden to Italy. While there, I met a collector in northern Italy who wanted the three fifty-six. He paid fifteen thousand dollars for it."

At that point, the Porsche went into a five-year restoration, and a few years ago, its current owner, a well-known Belgian collector, contacted Demosthenes about the car. "It turns out that it was the thirty-eighth three fifty-six constructed in the Stuttgart factory and reportedly the oldest 'known' coupe from Stuttgart," Demosthenes said.

Business is more difficult for this automotive archaeologist these days, as most of the great finds have been found. But like a good archaeologist, he keeps digging. Over his nearly four decades of discovering and purchasing more than one hundred 356 Porsches, the market has changed. "It's not hard to sell three fifty-sixes these days; it's just hard to find them. The three fifty-six supplies have dried up," he said. Today, he and his wife operate from a 1923 building on Scenic Route 30 in Mosier, Oregon, overlooking the Columbia River Gorge. The 4,500-square-foot business, called Route 30 Classics, houses a vintage Porsche showroom, a Porsche gift and memorabilia shop, and an adjoining gourmet ice cream and espresso shop.

"I am buying more early 911s now," he said regarding his current pursuit of Porsches. "As the age of the buyers get younger, it's the 1967 to 1973 Porsches they grew up dreaming about that they are buying. But that doesn't matter; it's all good."

THE FIRST '55 'VETTE

For at least four decades, Steve McCain has had a one-track mind for Corvettes. He decided early on that Chevrolet's fiberglass sports car was just his style, and he bought his first one—a 1965 model—while still in high school. While most of us would have been more than thrilled to impress our friends in the school parking lot with a (then) late-model 'Vette, McCain discovered his true automotive love.

"Back then, everyone who owned a Corvette automatically got a subscription to *Corvette News*," McCain said. "In one of those issues, they did a search for the oldest 1953 Corvette in existence. I thought the car looked really neat and decided I wanted one."

McCain lives in Summerfield, North Carolina, and the collector put the word out among his car friends in the nearby Greensboro area. He got a lead on a 1954 Corvette that was sitting behind a house, but the owner wouldn't sell.

"I was excited, but he wouldn't sell; he was saving it for his son," he said.

The 1953 and 1954 Corvettes were virtually identical cars. Both were powered by the Blue Flame six-cylinder engine and were equipped with a two-speed automatic transmission. And most were painted white. Both are rare; only three hundred 1953 models were manufactured and 3,640 1954 Corvettes were built.

In 1955, despite the optional V-8, only seven hundred Corvettes were built because they were hard to sell.

"When Ford introduced the Thunderbird in 1955, nobody wanted to buy a Corvette," McCain said. "They were actually getting ready to discontinue the Corvette model."

More than thirty years ago, McCain had unearthed another lead. "My friend Larry Melvin told me about a Corvette in Lexington, North Carolina."

McCain drove about an hour to see the car. It belonged to the brother of the owner of The Corvette Center, a specialty shop in Lexington. The '55 was parked behind the owner's parents' home nearby.

"The car was in pretty sad shape," McCain said. "My friend Bill Hampton went with me to check its credentials.

"I was told that on 1955 Corvettes, the serial number was on the steering column, but it wasn't," McCain said. "The owner didn't know either and just walked away.

"We finally found the VIN tag on the driver's side doorjamb. Imagine our surprise when we saw the numbers."

The VIN read VE55S001001, which translates thusly:

V: V-8 Engine.

E: Corvette Series.

55: Model year.

S: Saint Louis plant, where the car was produced.

Steve McCain followed up a lead on a 1955 Corvette, one of seven hundred built, which was near Lexington, North Carolina. The car was in pretty sad condition, but at the $500 asking price, he feels he got a pretty good deal. *Steve McCain*

001: All 1953–1955 Corvettes had the 001 designation.

001: The first car off the production line.

"I had always heard that Smokey Yunick got the first five Corvettes off the assembly line, but I guess not," he said.

McCain paid $500 for the car in 1970 and feels he got a pretty good deal.

Two years later, McCain heard of another early Corvette that was available, another 1955, for $1,000.

"It was in a junkyard in Wilkesboro [North Carolina] and was also in pretty sad shape," he said. "It had a big headrest that was molded into the rear trunk, holes in the frame, and holes where a small windscreen had been mounted. But it was a thousand dollars, and I just thought it was a botched-up car, and I didn't want another '55, so I didn't buy it."

To this day, McCain regrets this decision because eventually he found out the Corvette was built by Zora Arkus-Duntov, and he had used it extensively at GM's Arizona test track.

McCain was hardly left empty-handed though; he still had car number 001. The restoration of the first 1955 Corvette took four years. In 1976, he sold it for $10,000 to a collector who also had the first 1956 and the first 1957 Corvettes ever built.

Does he regret selling number 001? Sure, but McCain has owned many 'Vettes in his life, including one 1953, four 1954s, and the one 1955.

"If I still owned this car today, I think it would be more historically significant than the last 1967 big block, which got so much attention going into the [2007] Barrett-Jackson auction—and that was bid to more than six hundred thousand dollars," he said. "But these older cars just aren't as popular, so I'd say it would probably be worth two hundred thousand dollars."

An interesting side note, and a lesson on keeping in touch with people who own a car you'd like to acquire: Remember that first 1955 Corvette that McCain discovered behind a house in Lexington, but the guy was saving it for his son? Well in 1989, McCain received a call from the son, who was looking to purchase his first home and wanted to sell the Corvette. He sold the car to McCain for $8,000. McCain used it as a parts car for a customized 1953 'Vette he was restoring as a full custom (canted headlights, etc.).

That's not the end of the story yet. After the custom was completed, McCain turned his parts car into a hot rod. He widened the body and installed a late-model LT-1 drivetrain with a 700H automatic transmission. Then he painted it dark blue with scallops.

The moral? Corvettes are never scrapped—they are recycled!

LOW-MILEAGE MOUSE HOTEL

For some enthusiasts, the ultimate barn find is a Cobra (for me it was a 289); for others, it could be a Z28 Camaro or a Duesenberg. For John Forbes, of Denver, North Carolina, it has always been a Porsche 914/6.

Forbes is a well-known Porsche mechanic, restorer, and racer. He has worked exclusively on Porsches for forty-two years, the duration of his entire working life. As a teenager, he cut his teeth on a 911 at a gas station in Cherry Hill, New Jersey. In 1971, he became a mechanic at a Porsche dealership, specializing in engines and transmissions. His first exposure to racing came when he worked on Mark Donohue's Penske IROC Porsche at the dealership in 1974.

The racing bug had bit, and Forbes was hooked. He raced a series of six-cylinder 914 Porsches, occasionally beating factory pros such as Hurley Haywood and Bob Snodgrass from Brumos Porsche in Jacksonville, Florida. Eventually, Forbes opened his own Porsche repair facility—Black Forest Racing—and moved it to Denver, North Carolina, where he works on all Porsches, but prefers 914s.

For this Porsche barn-find story, though, we also need to mention a second Porsche mechanic named Wolfgang Schmidt. Schmidt worked in a Porsche dealership in southern New Jersey and ordered a brand-new, 1970 Irish Green 914/6 with black interior, appearance group, and steel wheels. He used the car sparingly on weekends for three years when, tragically, he was stricken with muscular dystrophy in his mid-thirties. In 1976, he passed away. His grieving widow parked the low-mileage Porsche in the garage next to a VW Beetle,

This is what a 1970 Porsche 914/6 with five thousand miles on it looks like after it's been stored for thirty-six years. Owner John Forbes believes it is the lowest mileage six-cylinder 914 in the world. *John Forbes*

where it sat untouched from 1976 to 2012. It was about that time that Forbes received a phone call from a friend, Karl, who operated a VW repair shop in New Jersey.

"Karl told me one of his customers was seventy-five years old and was selling her house," Forbes said. "He told me she had an old 914 Porsche in the garage that she needed to sell. He asked if I was interested."

It wasn't even a choice. Forbes hooked up his trailer and made the five-hundred mile trip to inspect the car as soon as he could. What he discovered was an Irish Green "mouse hotel." Mice, and probably chipmunks, had taken up residence in the car during its thirty-six-year slumber.

"The gas in the tank had turned to mud, and the interior smelled really bad," he said. "But the odometer showed a correct reading of only five thousand twenty miles."

He and friend Robert Fleischer bought the car, and finally Forbes realized his barn-find dream.

"Acorns were everywhere—in the glove box, in the heater channels, and under the gas tank," he said. "But the original tires held air, and the carpets cleaned up nicely. Thankfully, we were able to get the smell out."

Forbes removed the engine (which was stuck), cleaned it, and installed new rings. The dual Weber carbs only needed cleaning. The car was polished and displayed at several Concours d'Elegance events, winning the most original, lowest-mileage car at one. Porsche connoisseur Bob Ingram, chairman of the Pinehurst Concours in North Carolina, paid Forbes the highest compliment.

"He told me this could be the lowest mileage 914/6 in the world," Forbes said.

Maybe the one most appreciated by rodents too.

HARRY'S CURIOUS CUNNINGHAM

With only twenty-five Cunningham C-3s ever built, it's amazing that one appears in this barn-find book.

Classic car sleuth Chuck Schoendorf of Rowayton, Connecticut—the owner of a terrific collection of cars, including two Cunninghams—was on the lookout for C-3 number 5209, the fourth built between 1952 and 1953 out of a run of twenty-five at the Cunningham factory in West Palm Beach, Florida.

Number 5209 was the only missing Cunningham C-3, which after more than sixty years is amazing in itself. In 2011, Schoendorf made it his mission to either find the car or find out why it no longer existed.

Records show that the car was last owned by a Mr. Harry Sefried Jr. of Connecticut. Obituary archives showed Mr. Sefried died in 2005, but the obituary did not mention where he resided. It did, however, mention a daughter named Leslie Lockhard.

Schoendorf investigated and discovered that a Leslie Lockhard lived in Pennsylvania, and—BINGO!—there it was. "Yes, I still own the car, and it is still sitting behind my father's house in Connecticut," she said, rather surprised about the phone call. "But it's probably in pretty rough condition. It's been sitting outside for at least fifteen years."

Since the elderly Sefried was wheelchair-bound, he had kept the car in the backyard rather than in the nearby empty garage so he could keep an eye on it out of the window of his house. As a younger man, Sefried had a wild streak. He raced motorcycles, and when he purchased the C-3 in 1962, he

As Sefried aged, he looked out the window of his home as the car slowly deteriorated. Look carefully and you can see that the front suspension collapsed because the crossmember had deteriorated. *Tom Cotter*

purchased high-compression pistons, a high-lift camshaft, larger valves, and roller tappets directly from Briggs Cunningham. He intended to install the parts in his car but never got around to it.

"I remember Daddy used to drive me to school in the Cunningham," Leslie said.

After a few phone conversations, Schoendorf realized that he had discovered the only missing Cunningham C-3. But when he drove east across Connecticut to see the car, he was disappointed—the car was in terrible condition after being parked outside for so long, even though the empty garage stood just fifty feet away. Rust had penetrated so severely that the chassis' front crossmember had deteriorated, causing the front suspension to collapse.

And even though the Italian-made Vignale body was made of aluminum, much of the body's steel substructure was severely cancerous.

Leslie declined Schoendorf's offer to buy it, saying she would rather restore it in memory of her father. Schoendorf suggested, though, that instead of opting for an expensive restoration, he would be glad to oversee a less expensive, sympathetic refurbishment.

Before the repairs began, the car was displayed in the barn-find class at the Fairfield County Concours d'Elegance in Connecticut. "The car won the best barn-find class," Schoendorf said, "and the crowd flipped!"

Since then, number 5209 has been partially restored and displayed at a Cunningham Gathering at Lime Rock Park in Connecticut, where it won an award over several other concours-winning C-3s.

Leslie likes to think that her father, Harry, was watching it all from the window of his new residence, somewhere up there.

CHARLES GRANT'S 1970 DODGE SUPER BEE

I knocked on the door, and a woman answered. I told her I was writing a book about old cars and would like to discuss the Dodge in her driveway.

"I'll call my husband," she said. Her name was Gloria. "He's working on the roof around back."

Within a few minutes, we were talking with the Super Bee's owner, Charles Grant, who had bought the car new!

"I bought it right here in Salem in 1970," Charles said. "I traded in a 1964 Ford Galaxie XL500 with a three-hundred-ninety-cubic-inch plus about four thousand dollars for the car."

Charles's Super Bee has a 383-cubic-inch engine with a four-barrel carb and automatic transmission. Sitting there in his yard, the odometer registers 142,000 miles. It was last registered in 1996, so it had been sitting idle for over eighteen years.

"I saw that car at three o'clock in the morning on the dealer lot, so about a week later, I went back and bought it," he said.

When the car was new, it was red with a white vinyl roof and a reflective C-stripe along the side. Over the years, Charles had it repainted orange after it was involved in a minor collision. Charles told me that even though the car has the original rally wheels on it, at one time he ran chrome rims with ten-inch slicks on the back. I asked Charles if he had ever drag raced the car. No. Had he ever street raced it? No.

Charles bought this car new off the local Dodge dealership in Salem, Virginia. He admits to driving the car to 120 miles per hour "before the front end got light." *Michael Alan Ross*

"I've had it up to one hundred twenty miles per hour," he said. "But it gets light in the front end when you go that fast. And the drum brakes are not the best."

I asked if he was going to restore the Super Bee.

"At sixty-eight years old, I'm not sure I'm going to do anything with it, but my son is chomping at the bit for it," he said. "I just haven't decided to give it to him yet."

Charles said he had a couple of other old vehicles, like a 1956 Dodge three-quarter-ton truck his father bought from the original owner. The truck now belongs to Charles Grant Jr., Charles' son. Interestingly, Charles was driving this very truck the night he saw and fell in love with his Super Bee in 1970. The truck reminded me of what Timmy's father drove on the *Lassie* TV program.

He also showed us a couple of cars his younger brother owns, one he thinks is a 1967 Dodge Coronet R/T with a 400-cubic-inch, last driven in 1985, the other a Chevelle two-door hidden in the woods.

I had spent a couple of enjoyable hours walking through the woods with Charles, looking at old vehicles that were owned by him and his family. After checking myself for ticks, I jumped in the car and continued down the road. I just knew there had to be more old cars to be discovered.

After leaving Charles and his Super Bee, we decided to head south on less-traveled roads, specifically Highway 11, which was once a main north-south thoroughfare before the interstate was installed. We soon passed an old commercial garage that didn't appear to be in business. We stopped because we noticed several old pickup trucks behind the building. Brian and I peeked into one of the garage doors, and there was a partially disassembled 1937 Ford two-door sedan.

But nobody was around, and there was no phone number on the building, so we kept driving.

A little further down the road, we came across a used-car dealer that specialized in muscle cars. We figured they might know if there were any old cars in the area, but when we walked inside the showroom, nobody was there. We walked back into the shop, but there was nobody there either.

Hmmm. A dozen pristine old cars sat in the showroom. The lights and radio were on, but nobody was around. We figured that whoever was there that Saturday afternoon was probably out test-driving a car that he had been working on.

As we were leaving, a woman drove up and asked if we worked at the dealership.

We said no. Then she said, "Well, I'd like to sell my 1963 ½ Ford Falcon convertible I have at home and wanted to see if this dealership would like to buy it."

I asked what condition the Falcon was in, and she said perfect.

"My husband just had it restored last year."

I told her we were on the road to discover barn finds, not perfectly restored cars, so we said goodbye and continued on our way.

Charles' brother also had this 1966 Malibu sitting behind the house. *Michael Alan Ross*

A HAND-BUILT PROTOTYPE IN THE BASEMENT

When following up on a barn-find lead, it's best to keep your expectations low. For example, if you hear about an old Ford in a garage, it's best to assume it's a rusty Pinto, and not a GT40. This way, when the car turns out to only be a Mustang, you're happy.

Car-buying partners have always taken that approach. Friends Matt McSwain and Steve Goldin search out old race cars. Not the roundy-round stock cars you'd imagine a couple of country boys in the South would be attracted to, but significant sports cars. For instance, they own a couple of 24 Hours of Le Mans race cars and two John Greenwood Corvettes.

These easygoing guys have hunted for cars around the world—in France, Mexico, Ukraine, even Russia—so when they got a lead on a Porsche in nearby South Carolina, they couldn't get too excited. After all, how great could an old Porsche in sandy South Carolina be?

They inquired further and found out it was a midengine Porsche.

"Great," McSwain said. "It's probably just a 914 rust bucket." But they decided to investigate further. Their contact gave them the car's VIN number, so they Googled it and discovered it was a 916 model. Neither knew what a 916 was until they called a Porsche dealer and were told it was a very rare car.

"It doesn't make any difference what condition it is, just buy it," they were told.

"It was one of the most interesting places we've been to in our car-hunting careers," Goldin said. "Just a few old buildings, some with their roofs caved in,

The Porsche 916 looked presentable enough when the pair picked up the car but required a complete teardown and re-restoration, mostly because the rare prototype engine needed numerous custom and otherwise unobtainable components. *McSwain/Goldin*

and in the middle of nowhere. It was like an auto salvage yard but with some extraordinarily expensive cars."

The shop specialized in repairing British cars, so Rolls-Royces, Bentleys, Jaguars, and Aston Martins in various states of disrepair were parked around the property and in the buildings.

"The business owner, a Brit named Pip, would buy interesting old cars, fix them up, and never sell them," McSwain said. "Pip would even put new tires on them, then park them in the sand under an EZ-Up tent. There were hundreds of cars."

But the only car that McSwain and Goldin were interested in was the Porsche 916.

What they found in the basement of a building was one ugly Porsche. But the serial numbers checked out, and it was, in fact, an almost intact 916.

Exactly what is a 916? Don't feel embarrassed if you don't know, because only eleven were ever built.

The 1969 Porsche 916 was Porsche's first foray into midengine technology. Instead of the 914, which many of us are familiar with today, the 916 had aggressive flares front and rear, and it came equipped with either a honking 2.4- or 2.7-liter six-cylinder engine. But not the car that Goldin and McSwain were inspecting. It turns out *that* car was the very first 916 of the eleven built, the prototype, so it had a 2.9-liter engine out of an RSR race car.

"This was Porsche's first midengine car, designed on a clean sheet of paper, and hand-built piece by piece," explained Goldin.

Porsche used the prototype at auto shows around the world, repainting it frequently in different colors and changing the interior so it would appear that there were lots of 916 models, when, in fact, there was just this one show car.

When Porsche accountants did a cost analysis for the 916, they found that the retail cost would be more than the flagship 911, so the project was scrapped and ten of the 916s were sold off to racers or enthusiasts.

That very first car, though, was retained and had a second life within the Porsche family.

"Ferry Porsche's daughter, Carina, was given the car to drive to school," McSwain said.

After a few years as an academic commuter car, it was sold to a US Army doctor stationed in Germany. When he retired from the service sometime in the 1970s, he brought the car back with him to his native South Carolina.

"We were told it came to the States in the belly of a C-130 transport plane," McSwain said. "This is how the car got disconnected [from Porsche enthusiasts]. Nobody knew where the car went. There was no paper trail after the doctor brought it to the States. It had been totally under the radar since leaving the Porsche factory in the 1970s. When we Googled the serial number, it simply read: 'Lost 916.'"

The doctor brought the car for service to Pip and his mechanics, the same South Carolina location where forty years later Goldin and McSwain would discover the car.

"When the doctor passed away in the nineties, Pip bought the Porsche from the doctor's estate," Goldin said. "And he paid a lot of money for it at the time."

The new owner and his mechanics performed a quasi-restoration on the rare Porsche, but because it was a one-off prototype, they were unable to obtain correct replacement parts. So it was simply pushed into the basement of the building, semi-completed, where it would remain until 2014.

After purchasing the car, the partners began the research required for a correct restoration. Even though the car had been painted a number of colors and had a number of different interiors installed over the years, Goldin and McSwain decided to paint the car black with lime-green wheels.

"We believe this is the car's original color combination when it was first built," explained McSwain. "We had to have interior fabric produced that

The interior had been partially disassembled when an earlier restoration came to a halt. It then became a storage shed for random Porsche pieces. *McSwain/Goldin*

had the Porsche logo in white on a black background. Believe it or not, we discovered this car once had elephant hide interior."

McSwain and Goldin dismantled the Porsche in their own shop, then had components such as the engine and gearbox rebuilt by specialists.

Most of the restoration was performed by George Hussey, a 916 Porsche specialist in Atlanta, Georgia. Hussey used his own Porsche 916 as a guide to assemble the prototype and provided correct new old stock (NOS) parts from his own collection where needed.

"This car would have sold for at least eleven thousand dollars at a time when a Porsche 911 S sold for just sixty-two hundred," McSwain said. The numbers just didn't add up. So Porsche dumbed-down the 916 and made it into the 914, which mostly came with four-cylinder engines or standard 911 six-cylinders."

Since completion, Goldin and McSwain's 916 has been displayed at the Amelia Island Concours d' Elegance and the Porsche Museum in Atlanta, Georgia, and it was scheduled to appear on the *Jay Leno's Garage* TV program.

Not a bad outcome for a car that languished in a basement for so long.

"It's the least significant-looking car we own but the most historically significant car we own," Goldin said.

THE $3,000 FERRARI

Like so many enthusiasts of a certain age, Mark Gutzman spent his misguided youth pouring over the classified ads in the back of *Road & Track* magazine.

"I always dreamed about buying an old Ferrari but never thought I'd actually own one," said the Lexington, Kentucky, native.

But sometimes dreams do come true.

Gutzman had a friend who was a traveling salesman, selling calculators and typewriters. This was a different time, before laptop computers and cell phones.

The salesman drove a new Saab. Once, on the way to a sales call, he stopped at a Mercedes-Benz/Fiat/Saab dealership for an oil change. As he sat next to the dealership owner's desk waiting for his car to be serviced, he noticed a letter. Being the nosy type, he read it.

The letter was an inquiry to the dealership owner asking about the value of a 1964 Ferrari 250 GTE. The salesman was not really into Italian cars, but his good friend Mark Gutzman certainly was. Ever since Gutzman's first sports car, a 1500 Fiat, he was hooked.

So his salesman friend called and told Gutzman there was apparently an old Ferrari in the neighboring county. Now Gutzman was on the hunt.

He called a friend who worked in that county and asked, "Do you know anyone who might own an old Ferrari?"

"Would it have a long hood?" his friend asked.

His friend gave him the address for a pharmacist who lived in nearby Camargo, Kentucky. The next time Gutzman was in the area, he stopped at the address.

To buy even the cheapest front-engine, 12-cylinder Ferrari today might cost one hundred times the $3,000 he spent for the mouse-infested field-find. *Mark Gutzman*

And there, like a dream, was a Ferrari sitting in the farm field. How could this be?

It turns out the car had a fuel leak, so it was pushed into the field so the gas stink wouldn't permeate the farmer's house.

"This was in 1980, and the value of Ferraris had not yet skyrocketed," Gutzman said. "The farmer had a Datsun B210 parked in the garage while the silver Ferrari sat in the field. It had become a high-class mouse hotel.

"I had found out that the owner had traded his Mercedes-Benz 190 SL for the Ferrari in the seventies," Gutzman added. In fact, he had found the original November 22, 1971 newspaper advertisement for the car: "Ferrari 2-door, V-12 engine, 5-speed, gray. $3,995." Gutzman and the owner just couldn't come to terms on the value of the non-functioning Ferrari, so Gutzman left.

About a year later, he was thinking about what might have happened to the Ferrari, so he called the owner's phone number. The owner's wife answered the phone.

"I said I was still interested in the car, and that I would give them 'three' for the car," he said.

She asked, "You mean three hundred?"

"No, three thousand."

By the time he got home from work that day, Gutzman had a message on his phone that the pharmacist was indeed interested in selling the car. Gutzman drove there the following Saturday and the two shook hands on the deal, $3,000.

One week later, Gutzman borrowed his father-in-law's truck and rented a U-Haul car trailer to pick up the car. With a jack, tools, and a battery, he loaded the car and dragged it home.

"I parked it in my driveway but covered it with a tarp so my neighbors wouldn't complain," he said.

Performing some basic diagnosis, he determined the electric fuel pump was faulty and the brake master cylinder needed rebuilding. During a business trip to Atlanta, he stopped at Ferrari specialist FAF and purchased a brake cylinder rebuilding kit, a fuel pump, and an assortment of banjo fitting gaskets, which would solve the fuel leak that had originally sentenced the car to solitary confinement the field.

After installing a new battery, Gutzman was able to start the mighty twelve-cylinder engine, but only one bank of cylinders was firing. He diagnosed the problem as a bad ignition coil, so a trip to the local auto parts store and the purchase of a Chevy coil solved that.

"All the cylinders fired after that," he said. "That car was bullet-proof. Once I got it running, I never had another problem with it."

Gutzman never drove the car daily but used it frequently on weekends for drives to sports car events in the area.

"Around town, it felt heavy, like driving a 1953 Chevy truck," he said. "But once it started rolling, it was sweet."

After several years, Gutzman sold the Ferrari. Does he have any regrets about that?

"I sold it for six thousand," he said. "And I bought a two-liter Alfa Romeo. I doubled my money; I thought I had made a great deal."

TWO CANADIAN FREEBIES

I'm often asked: What are the best methods of finding old cars? My first suggestion is always to make friends with people who can go onto private property legally.

At seminars, I suggest that folks make friends with landscapers, UPS and FedEx delivery people, and police officers. These folks can travel farther onto the property than you can see from the road.

I recently spoke with one of those lucky people. Kirby Bernier works for a gas utility in Edmonton, Alberta, Canada. He is often on the road in the rural Northwest Territory, performing maintenance and checking for leaks in the gas pipes that run across residential and agricultural properties.

"We have to go out and perform maintenance on the lines every two years," the fifty-year-old said. "Usually, it's just greasing the valves so they remain operational.

"And every year, I'd go next door to this property and see a little red sports car sitting next to a barn in the distance. But I didn't want to trespass on this private property, so I usually went the long way around to reach the valves."

One day in 2013, while Kirby was servicing the gas lines, a black pickup truck pulled up.

"Hey, you can just go across my property," the man said. "It's a lot easier than going the long way around."

Kirby thanked the man and talked to him for a few minutes.

"I've been servicing those valves for about nine years and have always wondered about that little sports car next to your building," Kirby said. "Is it an MG?"

"No, that's one of those Volkswagen kit cars," the landowner explained. "I won it in a poker game back in 1971. I dragged it home, and it has been sitting there ever since. Come spring, I think I'm just going to dig a big hole and bury it."

"If you want it, you can have it."

Kirby was elated. He and the owner walked over to look at it up close.

"Yeah, back when I got it, the thing ran, but it never had a hood," the owner said.

"Sure, I'll take it," Kirby said.

The two shook on the deal. Kirby agreed to come back in the fall when the landowner would have the trees down around it.

Several months went by, and Kirby returned with a rented flatbed trailer behind his pickup.

The landowner had another appointment so was not able to assist Kirby with loading the car.

"I rented a basic flatbed utility trailer, so it did not have a winch on the front," he said. "I only had a simple come-along. With the car having three frozen wheels, I spent quite a while loading it by myself."

When he finally got the car home, Kirby went on his computer and tried to figure out what kind of car he had just dragged home. Details that differentiated this VW-based sports car from others was that it did not have a conventional Beetle floorpan but instead was mounted on a purpose-built tube-frame chassis.

He eventually stumbled upon a website, www.devinspecial.com, and realized that he was now the owner of a Devin D, a late-1950s or early-1960s fiberglass special. Some were built from kits, but most were manufactured at the Devin factory and sold as turn-key cars with either a VW or Porsche engine.

Devins were conceived and designed by the company's founder, Bill Devin. Devin produced a series of fiberglass sports cars that could be built on a variety of chassis and powered by engines from manufacturers such as VW/Porsche, Corvair, Borgward, Triumph, Austin Healey, and all the way up to Chevy V-8s. Initially, the cars were built as turn-key cars, but eventually Devin sold kits as well. The cars were mostly street driven but were also road raced and drag raced.

Kirby's Devin D is powered by a 1964 VW forty-horsepower engine, but since everything else on the car is from a 1958 VW, he believes the original thirty-six-horsepower 1958 engine was likely swapped out in the 1960s for the later powerplant.

The farmer who built this bike as a teen said that it never felt right because of the raised handlebars. "If you want it, take it" was music to Kirby's ears. *Kirby Bernier*

"I discovered that only forty-nine Devin Ds were built between 1958 and 1963," he said. "Mine is also one of the first ones built because it has squared-off fenders. Interestingly, today there are only two known examples of these very early Devin Ds, and they are both in Canada."

Kirby has spent five years researching his Devin, and he's not sure what to do next. It's missing the hood, and it certainly requires a very thorough restoration.

One thought is to display it at the Reynolds-Alberta Museum for a year or so. Maybe by that time, he would have the time and financial resources to complete the restoration. On the other hand, he may decide to sell it.

"I'm on the fence about keeping it or selling it," he said. "It costs me nothing, so I have nothing to lose. We'll see."

Kirby said there are probably many cars in the far northern reaches of Canada. He noted that people would regularly drive cars far up north, and then when they broke down, they just left them there.

"I grew up in the Yukon, about six hundred miles north from where I live now," he said. "When I was a kid, I would ride around in my sister's boyfriend's four forty Road Runner. When he blew the engine, he just parked it in his parent's backyard."

Kirby told me about another car, a Pontiac Judge convertible, that was purchased by a friend.

"The owner wanted three hundred dollars for it, but my friend got it for only two hundred."

He showed me a photo of that car, which is now restored. It was an amazing find.

Kirby also told me the story of his free chopper motorcycle.

"I was repairing a leak in the gas line of this guy's property," he said. "He came out of the house and we were talking. I asked him about the chopper I saw hanging on the wall inside the building.

"I asked, 'Is that a Honda?'

"The man said, 'Well, yes, it's a CB350. I built it when I was a kid in the seventies. I grew up in a town of about twenty people, and a friend of mine had a welder. So even though we didn't know what we were doing, we built it in his shop. 'But with those high handlebars, it was never comfortable to ride.'"

Kirby was just about to ask if it was for sale, when the man said, "If you want it, you can have it."

So Kirby dragged it home and got it running.

"I've had it about two years, but I guess I would sell it if someone was interested in it," he said.

Kirby went on to tell me that the motorcycle riding season in the Northwest Territory is very sort, but when it is riding season, he prefers his other bike instead. It's a 1983 Honda V65 Magna.

"It's one of the fastest bikes built," Kirby said. "It has one hundred fifteen horsepower and can run the quarter-mile in 10.97 seconds."

When I spoke to Kirby, it was in January. I asked what the temperature was outside.

"Last week, it was minus forty degrees Fahrenheit, but next week it's going to warm up to only minus twenty-five degrees," he said.

A heat wave!

SNOWBALL BISHOP'S FIELD OF FORDS

"Brother, at one time I had seventeen 1940 Ford coupes," he said. "I'd make race cars out of them. Right now, all I got are these old Fords here, some in the other building and in the field, and I got the old race car in the other shop."

I quickly realized that our visit to Snowball Bishop's house was not going to be a short one. I told Snowball, "We saw your field from the interstate." He told us that sometimes folks see his cars from the highway and just climb over the fence and walk on in, leaving their cars sitting on the interstate!

"I'm eighty-five-years-old, brother," he said. "I've been collecting cars my whole life."

Snowball invited us into one of his garages to see a couple of his favorite cars. He was obviously a Ford man, and, as we would discover, an enthusiast of the 390-cubic-inch FE engine. He lifted up the car cover and revealed a pristine white 1964 Ford two-door hardtop.

"This one has a three ninety in it with three hundred horsepower," Snowball said. "I've had this one since 1968."

He led us to another covered car in the garage. As he lifted the cover, it revealed another 1964 Ford, this time a brilliant blue Galaxie. I jokingly asked him, "Is 1964 the year you were born?" He laughed and said he wished that were the case.

"Now this one here, I tore all the way [apart] about fifteen years ago," he said. "This one here is a three ninety, four-speed car. I didn't like the factory metallic blue, so I changed it to this color. I restored this one myself."

I asked him about the cars in the field behind his barn. "Are those cars all parts cars?"

"A lot of them are parts cars, but some of them out there can be put back on their feet," he said. "I brought in another 1963 and a 1964 just the other day. And I bought a 1963 convertible that some other boy started on, but cancer got him, so I bought it."

Then he pointed to a 1965 Ford his son had recently dragged home.

"It's a 1965 Ford that had been put up eighteen years ago," he said. "It's got a solid body on it, and it's a three ninety car. The frame is good under it. It had no engine in it, so [the owner] started out wanting two thousand dollars for the car. My son Jimmy offered him fifteen hundred for the car, and he took it home."

Then Snowball showed us some photos of himself as a younger man. "Is that you?" my travel buddy Brian Barr asked.

"Yes, that's me when I was racing," he said. "I have a whole house full of them [photos]."

Modified Racer

Apparently, Snowball had been quite a driver on the NASCAR Modified circuit back in the day.

"I've got my old '37 Ford race car in the other garage. Would you like to see it?" I thought Brian was going to burst at the seams with excitement. As we walked toward the garage, Snowball got reminiscent. "Now this place here has a lot of history," he said. "I think Daddy put this building up in the 1950s. At the time, it was all we had. We didn't have any money back then. It's a wonder that this old building hasn't burned up three or four times. We used to heat it with an old potbelly stove that was in the corner.

"The only power we had was to run a power cord from our house across the street."

As he opened the door, sunlight shone on the race car that had been a part of his life for so many years. "One time when we rebuilt that old car, we put a Chevy frame under it," he said.

I asked when he purchased the car. He said it was so long ago he couldn't remember. "I had so many coupes back then, I don't know when I bought this one.

"But if I'm not mistaken, I think I got this car from the Jackson boys. I think the last time I raced it was in 1973 or 1974, I can't remember."

Snowball said that he built the coupe in this very garage.

"Did it race with a Ford engine?" I asked.

Snowball told us he initially raced with a series of modified flathead engines and usually finished in the top five against the more modern overhead-valve Chevy engines in the 1960s. He talks proudly of a couple of Crossfire flatheads he ran. Crossfire engines fire two sparkplugs at once. After flatheads, he tried a Holman-Moody-built 312-cubic-inch engine, then a 406-cubic-inch Ford, but ultimately decided to switch to Mopar engines. In later years, the car ran with a 413-cubic-inch Chrysler engine with a four-speed gearbox, but that changed when he bought a load of engines and parts from Petty Enterprises.

Petty Connection

"I'm telling you the honest truth," Snowball said. "I drove up to Richard Petty's house with my old pickup, and maybe I had one thousand dollars in my pocket. Old man Lee Petty was sitting there in a chair and said, 'How are you boys getting along?'

"'Mr. Lee,' I said. 'I heard you were selling some good four twenty-six stuff, and we're here to buy it. We're looking for the good Stage Three heads and the good intakes. My four thirteen runs good, but it won't beat the Chevys anymore.'

"Lee said, 'See that pile of stuff there in the corner? There's three engines there and enough parts to build two more. If I'm not mistaken, there are six Stage Three heads in there, and all sorts of camshafts, pistons, rods.'

"Richard had gone to the Hemi engine by then, so he was selling all the four twenty-six Wedge stuff," Snowball said. "So Lee says, 'What would you give me for it? Would you give one thousand dollars for all that stuff in the corner?' I said, 'Mr. Lee, you wouldn't lower that just a little so I have enough money to get home, would you?' He died laughing and took nine hundred dollars for everything.

"Later I ran a four hundred forty-cubic-inch Chrysler engine in the car," he said. "The engine for it is out of it now and is sitting next to it on the floor. I turn it over every week."

Before we left the old garage, Snowball told us that, besides working on the old stock car, he also used the garage as a makeshift poker parlor.

"We'd start playing cards, and about one or two o'clock in the morning, my wife would start cutting out the lights by pulling the power cord out of the socket up at the house. That was the time to go on home. Those were the good old days."

The Coupe Today

"I don't want to put the motor back in it until the car is painted," he said. "I told Jimmy, 'Hey, you better get on the ball and get this thing painted. Daddy might not be here too much longer. I'd like to hear that thing run again.' You wouldn't believe how many people tried to buy that old car off of me. Ray Evernham wanted to buy it."

As we walked to his other garage, Snowball said that when I-77 was built, it cut his farm in two. He said he still owns about one hundred acres of land on one side and about thirty-nine acres on the side where his home and cars sit.

Snowball's father had scrimped and saved and bought the farm back in the 1930s during the Depression. He explained that he and his siblings were raised in the family's old home place at the lower end of the field. There used to be an old schoolhouse on the property that his mother attended.

Snowball said he acquired an additional two-acre lot below the family property years ago, which is where he used to keep his cars: "I used to keep that lot plum full of old cars; I had 1937, '39, '40 Fords up in there and plum up into the 1950s, coupes, pickups. I just phased them out; people bought them up, and I couldn't find no more."

As we walked past my Woody, he stopped to admire it. I told him I bought it in 1969 when I was fifteen years old. He wanted to look under the hood, but I told him I didn't want to ruin his day.

"You have a Chevy in there, don't you?" he asked as I reached for the hood latch.

"Yes, I do," I said. "Even though I'm a Ford guy, I couldn't say no to this LS1 engine."

"Mmmmmm, mmmmm, that sure is sweet," he said.

The next garage, like the previous one, was loaded with 1963 and 1964 Ford pieces: grilles, trim, emblems, headlight doors. "I've got a field full of 1964 Fords. And that old house over there is filled with parts and junk, Lord have mercy."

Huge 1963 and '64 Ford Stash

"You wouldn't believe that they come from everywhere looking for 1963 and 1964 Ford stuff off of me," Snowball said. "They'll stop over there on the interstate and walk across the pasture to find me.

"They'll say, 'We didn't know how to get here.'

"I sell the boys some things, because you can't find these old parts anymore. I've sold Larry McClure a lot of stuff over the years. He's the boy who owned

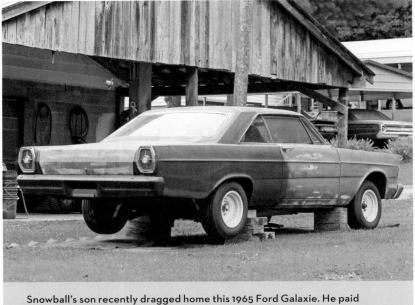

Snowball's son recently dragged home this 1965 Ford Galaxie. He paid $1,500 and hopes to restore the car, which was originally powered by a 390.
Michael Alan Ross

the [NASCAR] team that Sterling Marlin and Ernie Irvan drove for. He has some old Fords and was restoring some old Galaxies back. He called me the other day and was looking for a console and a set of bucket seats for an XL.

"I sell cars and parts when I can. I try to help the boys out. If I got it, I'll let you have it. If I don't have it, they'll just have to go on down the road to someone else."

We walked toward a newer steel building. Snowball said that he recently had it constructed for some of his nicer cars. As we raised the door, our eyes instantly went toward a beautiful 1963 Ford Galaxie convertible.

"It came from North Wilkesboro," Snowball said. "I guess I'm the second owner on it. Everybody who sees this sharp old '63 wants to buy it. It is a factory four-speed car, and it is unrestored.

"I bought it about five years ago. I bought it from a boy named Jimmy Williams who had a stroke, and because it's a four-speed car, he couldn't shift it anymore, so I went over and bought it from him."

AUTOMOTIVE JURASSIC PARK

In Maryland, we followed my friend Chuck Goldborough from highways to rural roads until we came across a residential yard that was littered with dozens of interesting old cars: old Divco milk trucks, Corvairs, East European Trabants—all spread across the front yard.

This was amazing. We parked our cars and walked around with our mouths gaping. I honestly don't know if I've ever seen a collection quite like this. I have an eclectic automotive taste, so to me seeing collections of only Thunderbirds or Jaguars is not half as interesting as this.

Ready? Yugos, Chevys (1955, '57), Trabants (passenger cars, Jeep types, and wagons), Caddys, Corvairs (sedans, vans, and pickups), VWs (Beetles and buses), Fords (domestic, English Prefects, and Zephyrs), a Plymouth Barracuda, an International Harvester, a mid-sixties T-Bird roadster, and more and more and more.

And that is just what I could see in the front and side yard and through the fence. There were many, many more cars in the backyard I could not see because it was blocked by all the bamboo! (Remember bamboo?) I had to talk to the owner. I knocked on the door and met Andrew Annen. He said his father, Mike, owned the cars, and that he was at work.

"I'll call him and see when he'll be home," said Andrew as he walked back into the house.

When he came back, he said his father would be home after 7 p.m. and that he'd be glad to meet us. But until then, Andrew would be glad to show us

225

some of the cars in the front and side yards. We started out looking at the Trabants, a brand that was manufactured in Eastern Europe during the Cold War. They were two-cylinder, two-cycle, air-cooled, and front-wheel drive. And they had the reputation of being smoky and slow.

"These have metal subframes and a body made of cotton fiber," Andrew said. "They take cotton—basically old clothes—and press it with resin and it turns into a hard, almost plastic-like material."

Andrew said they can smoke badly if oil is mixed incorrectly. In reality, they are like the two-stroke engines in a Lawn Boy lawn mower.

"It's like a weed wacker," he said. "The earlier ones smoke a lot. My father has been bringing them in from out of the country." He pointed to a Trabant military vehicle, which I just could not imagine going to war with.

"My dad's been into Trabants since about 2004," he said. When I asked what type of car his father drives every day, I was surprised to find out it was a Mitsubishi electric car. "He had been into big American cars, but then he started to get into smaller European stuff," Andrew said. "Now Trabants are his next big adventure."

Andrew told me that Trabants are pretty reasonably priced. "Depending on their condition, about three thousand dollars for a running daily driver. They are EPA and DOT exempt because they are more than twenty-five years old."

Michael aimed his camera over the fence, and this is what he saw! Let me see—right to left, I think it's a Trabant, a Vespa, and a Model A Ford Deluxe cabriolet. *Michael Alan Ross*

This was a serious find, and I was so glad Mike agreed to talk to us. I gave Andrew a copy of my 50 *Shades of Rust* book, which had just been released. "Here, give this to your father," I said. "We'll be back after seven o'clock."

We left with Chuck for a terrific meal a few miles down the road at a place called the Manor Tavern. Great place in Monkton, Maryland, smack dab in the middle of horse country. We had some great food; I had the baby back ribs with their special homemade barbecue sauce, which had quite a kick! And there was a kicking bluegrass band playing as well. It was a neat place, and some of the patrons at the bar approached us to talk about our Woody in the parking lot.

Almost two hours later, it was getting dark and was time for us to go back to Mike's house so we could meet the man in person.

Chuck said goodbye, having spent almost two entire days with us. He needed to go back home to spend some quality time with his family. Before I said goodbye to Chuck, I reminded him that I would still like to see that barn full of old Porsches while I was in the area. He promised to find out about their status and call us in the morning. With that, we headed back up the road to Mike's house.

I knocked on the door and Mike invited me inside. He had been reading the 50 *Shades* book, so he had a good idea of who I was before we met. Even though it was dark out—almost 8 p.m. by now—he offered to take us on a tour of his backyard and buildings. He provided the flashlights.

But first he wanted to check out my Woody. Mike was a real car guy. He started to discuss the Trabants. He said his son Mathew was operating the website www.trabantusa.com and that there are close to a hundred members nationwide.

"It was actually Tom Brokaw that got me into Trabants," he said. "We had been watching the news about the Berlin Wall coming down, and I became intrigued with the little cars."

Eventually, Mike was bringing home shipping containers full of Trabants from Europe. He said he's paid as little as $25 for them, plus $9 customs fees. He could stack six in a container. He's traveled to England, Germany, Poland, and Hungary on Trabant-buying trips.

Okay, enough with the Trabants. What else did Mike have?

"My first car was a 1969 Chevelle that I wrapped up and kept on rebuilding," he said. "Then I bought another Chevelle, which was an SS 396. I still have that car in the barn.

"My first old car I found in 1978 while riding around during high school, and it was a 1950 Buick Sedanette. It was a straight-eight with a Dynaflow transmission.

"The gas mileage sucked. Then I got into Divco milk trucks for a while. I bought a bunch and have rented them out for movies. I bought eleven for twenty-two hundred dollars from a laundry near D.C. that was closing. I made money renting them out, and when the movie was over, I sold one truck for three thousand dollars. I still have about nine left." Mike told me about the challenges of owning that many cars in a residential area.

He must register each vehicle with Maryland Historic tags and has to deal occasionally with police officers who decide to walk through his property to inspect license plate tags.

Other cars on Mike's property: a Model T, a Model A, a '47 Chevy Coupe (semi hot rodded), a DKW (freshly restored), a '51 Chevy hardtop with Cadillac fins, a Renault, an Oldsmobile, 1953 and 1954 Chryslers, a Fiat (couple of 850s), an International tow truck, a 1961 Buick Skylark convertible, a Citroen 2 CV, and on and on.

Most of the cars in the rear of Mike's property were buried in a bamboo forest, which hides most of the cars until you are right on top of them. Mike said that if he cuts the bamboo, it grows back quickly. He's given up on trying to keep it mowed down.

And to make this discovery even more insane, Mike has another 150 cars in a building on a piece of property he owns in West Virginia! I asked him how he planned to deplete his collection one day; would he have an auction or sell them off one by one?

"I guess when I go, the old lady is going to have a big junk sale," he said with a big smile.

To me, this was the most significant find of the fourteen-week adventure that was *Barn Find Road Trip*, and one of the best finds of my life. Mike knew he had the car sickness real bad, and joked about it. He was a great guy and was so kind in allowing us to see his collection. He said that he never gives tours of his property, so we felt very lucky.

I seriously could have spent another eight or ten hours walking through that bamboo forest and listening to Mike's stories. This was a discovery that car geeks dream about stumbling upon once in their lives. It was a great adventure, and I hope to come back for another visit when I am in the area.

We headed off to our hotel. It had been a long, long day. Time to call it quits. I believe I could write a book just about Mike's collection. What a day.

BARN-FIND FREEWAY: MOTHER LODE NO. 1

We were finishing up shooting photos of an Victress coupe when I received a call from Eric Stanczak, the man who owned the fenced-in yard of old cars a few blocks from where we were at the former Packard plant. He said he was running a little late and asked us to meet him in front of his yard at 11:30 a.m. instead. With a little more time to kill, we just went driving around for a while, taking in Detroit's urban sites. We met some other folks who had old cars, but none with interesting stories.

At 11:30, we pulled the Woody up to the curb on a very busy industrial block, across the street from a huge auto wrecking yard. Stanczak had not yet arrived. We snooped at the cars we could see through the fence, but with rows of razor wire across the top, no way was I going over to get a closer look.

A little while later, a bright yellow 1955 Chevy hot rod pulled up. It was Stanczak, and he had brought his full-of-life twelve-year-old granddaughter, Autumn, with him.

"I started working on cars when I was about eleven years old," Stanczak said. "I grew up very close to where we are standing. My first car was a '57 Plymouth that didn't run—I got it from my uncle. My dad and I worked on it and got it running, so I sold it and bought another one. It just kept going from there."

Stanczak worked in a body shop for fifteen years and later started a trucking company.

This 1949 Chrysler coupe was particularly attractive. The body is solid, the original interior (which is under seat covers) is excellent, and it runs. *Michael Alan Ross*

"People got to know me, so if they wanted to get rid of a car, they would call me," he said. "Then, when they opened the auto shredder across the street, and steel was going for three hundred dollars per ton, a lot of these wrecker drivers were dragging old cars out of garages and bringing them across the street to be crushed. A lot of the guys would bring the older cars over here first, and I'd give them more than the scrap yard was offering."

In other words, Stanczak stood in front of his building and was offered old cars every day. A freeway of junk cars—barn finds—beat a path right to his front door! Sounds like my fantasy.

"These days, most of the wrecker drivers know I'm into old cars, so they give me the first shot at the cars they drag in. For instance, I bought this car as it was being dragged in to be crushed," he said, pounding on the fender of a white Lincoln MKIII. "It has a custom paint job, Kelsey-Hayes wire wheels. It was being scrapped because the transmission was going out on it. It runs great, but it only drives backwards. It just doesn't go forward. It only has sixty thousand miles on the odometer."

We looked at Stanczak's barn-find collection. He told me that he keeps his nicer cars at home. In addition to the '55 Chevy he drove here, he has a 1930 Model A roadster, a 1936 Chevy coupe, a 1975 Triumph TR6, a 1933 dual-cowl, dual-side-mount touring car, and another '36 Chevy street rod that was built in the 1950s. Stanczak guided us through his two buildings, which were loaded with better cars than the ones in the fenced yard.

"Some of these cars I've had for thirty years," he said as we made our way around the very tightly packed and very dusty buildings. This was a car hunter's heaven, but it sure was dirty business.

"I like to buy them and get them running," he said. "That's just what I enjoy doing. But I'll start working on one car, then another one will show up, then another, and before you know it, they are just piling up and I don't have a chance to work on them."

Just then, Autumn asked if she could speak into my tape recorder.

"There are hundreds and hundreds of cars that my grandfather needs to sell," she said. "So come down and buy some cars from us at a good price." She might have a future as a car salesperson!

There was a 1952 Ford Victoria that Stanczak said runs well. And there was a 1949 Chrysler coupe that also runs and drives.

"The body is real solid and the seats are covered, but the original upholstery is like new," he said.

Talk about rare—this 1953 Buick convertible is complete and in very good condition. It has power everything and a Nailhead V-8 powerplant.
Michael Alan Ross

It's a shame that interest in vintage cars such as this 1928 Buick is waning, because solid examples like this are amazing works of mechanical art and can be purchased for reasonable prices. *Michael Alan Ross*

One Mopar from the muscle car era was a 1964 Dodge Polara coupe. "It has a high-performance three eighty-three, headers, a new four-barrel, and a push-button Torqueflite transmission," he said.

That seemed like a no brainer. With its black-and-white checkered grille, it seemed to me to resemble a Dodge Ramcharger drag car, fresh from the strip.

"It's been in a garage since 1969, and there is no rust on it. It runs and shifts fine."

I pointed to a sharp Buick convertible a few feet away.

"That's a 1953 Nailhead V-8 with full power," Stanczak said. "Power top, power seats, power brakes, power steering, power everything. But it needs a new master cylinder, so it doesn't have any brakes."

Next to the Buick was a 1957 Oldsmobile with wire wheels. It looked hot rodded.

"It has dual quads on a three hundred ninety-four–cubic-inch engine," he said. "It runs and drives. It has a little rust in the trunk, but that's all the rust I could find."

Then Autumn came back for round two with my tape recorder.

"Hello, this is Autumn, and I want to tell all the fans that you should come over to my poppa's warehouse and look around at all our old cars. We're going to have a, um, an auction. Just call us and you can look around. Bye."

I really enjoyed these periodic commercials.

We walked over to the other building, where a 1957 Chevy two-door hardtop sat right next to the front door. It had been hot rodded, with a Hurst shifter poking through the floor that was attached to a Muncie four-speed transmission. Sprinkled around elsewhere inside the tightly packed Building No. 2 was a Triumph TR7, a 1958 Chevy half-ton panel truck, and another three-quarter-ton.

After a couple of hours of getting filthy looking at Stanczak's cars, we all decided we were getting hungry. It was almost 3 p.m., so I offered to buy lunch for Stanczak and Autumn. He recommended a restaurant in Hamtramck, the Polish section of Detroit, and told me that his grandparents moved to Detroit from Poland and never spoke a word of English. His grandfather went to work at the Dodge Main plant for his entire career. That plant is now a GM factory.

In the restaurant, I asked him if any of his cars had interesting stories. He told us about one that was covered up when we visited, so we hadn't seen it.

"A guy came in to see my cars and we started talking," Stanczak said. "This was back in the 1990s. He said, 'I have an old car in my garage, a 1949 Cadillac.' So I told him I would like to see it, and I drove to his house in Ferndale. I looked in the garage, and, sure enough, there was a 1949 Caddy. I opened the hood and it had a motor. It was a four-door sedan. I opened and shut all the doors, and they all felt good. It only had one flat tire."

The good news is that this 1965 Buick Wildcat is rare and complete. The bad news is that the convertible top has been missing for years, so the floors are non-existent. Got a solid sedan as a parts donor? *Michael Alan Ross*

Stanczak was interested. He asked the man how much he was asking for it; the man said it belonged to his mother, and she wanted it out of the garage. Make him an offer. His dad had parked it in here, he waxed it back in 1969, and it had not left the garage since. Stanczak told his wife, who was sitting in their car, he didn't really want the car, that he was not fond of '49 Cadillacs, but he felt he needed to pursue it.

"So I made an offer. The guy said, 'I'll go ask my mom.'"

Stanczak could see the old woman looking out the window of the house. She was about ninety years old. He could see her head shake back and forth, like she was telling her son no, but when the man came back outside, he said his mother agreed.

Stanczak brought it back to his building, not knowing whether it ran or not. "I messed around with the points a little bit to get it running and drove it around that whole summer! Everything worked great; it ran and shifted just fine. I never even changed the spark plugs on it."

While we talked, Autumn was keeping Michael Alan Ross entertained. She asked if she could see a photo of his wife, Danielle.

"Oh, she's beautiful," Autumn said. "Is she a model?" Just then, Autumn's spaghetti was delivered to the table. And her fried chicken too. And bread

This 1941 Dodge sedan is surprisingly solid and complete. Stanczak didn't give me a price for it, but everything he has is for sale and fairly priced. *Michael Alan Ross*

This 1958 Chevy Apache panel truck is one of two Stanczak owns. This one, which is a 1/2-ton, has a hot-rod drivetrain. The other, a 3/4-ton, is stock. *Michael Alan Ross*

and butter. Plus she picked food off her grandfather's plate. She had quite an appetite! I asked her what grade she would enter next year.

"I'm going into seventh grade, and I have a lot of books to read over the summer," she said.

I asked her if she had a lot of friends.

"Yes, I have four thousand friends." Then she asked me if I wanted to know who one of her Facebook friends was. I said yes. She declared, "Taylor Swift is my friend," just as sassy as could be.

I asked Stanczak about the 1956 Ford in his building.

"I had a friend who cleaned out all those old houses that were foreclosed on in downtown Detroit when the market crashed," he said. "He called me up when he found it in a garage and asked if I wanted it. I said, 'Let me come over and look at it.' It ran, so I bought it and drove it home. I've probably had it eight years now."

Stanczak told me about some of the cars that are towed into the scrap yard across the street.

"One time a guy was driving in a 1997 Mazda of some sort," he said. "He told me he was moving back to Africa and didn't need it anymore; he wasn't coming back. So I asked, 'What's wrong with it?'

"'Nothing,' he said.

"'Does it have a clear title?'

"'Yes.'

"So I drove it around the block and asked how much money he wanted for it. I bought it and gave it to my other granddaughter, who drove it for years."

Apparently scrapping cars is an alternative to selling them in this Detroit neighborhood.

"One guy scrapped his car for rent money," he said. Sad.

When we finished lunch, we went back to the shop. Michael was working his magic with amazing photos of the cars, and I walked around with Stanczak looking at the cars in his two fenced-in yards. Because I dig old flathead-powered Fords, I asked him about the 1951 Merc he had sitting outside.

"A garage collapsed and the guy wanted to tear it down," he said. "So he offered me a package deal for both cars.

The green-and-white '57 Oldsmobile on the left is a real cool car. The dual-quad 394-cubic-inch engine runs well, and the car rides on chrome wire wheels. *Michael Alan Ross*

"The other car was a 1967 Chevy Impala, but when I pulled it out, the car broke in half, so I junked it. The Mercury came without one fender but is amazingly complete and solid. I had to install a carburetor on it, but it just runs beautifully; you can't even hear it run. It has a rebuilt flathead engine with an overdrive transmission."

As we walked around looking at cars, Autumn was using one of Michael's extra cameras, pretending she was a professional photographer as well.

As we stood on the sidewalk, a nonstop stream of trucks was dragging cars through the gate of Strong Steel to be crushed.

Stanczak told me that Strong Steel was the world's largest car shredder.

"That is state of the art," he said. "They put a car in there, and the machine shreds it and separates all the metals, the steel from the aluminum from the brass, nickel. It even has a coin collector in case there is any change under the seats. And if there are any human remains in the car, such as a body in the trunk, the machine senses it and shuts everything down."

Before we left, there was one more car I wanted to find out about—the 1952 Packard Clipper that was sitting behind the fence.

"I bought that Packard and a Cougar at the same time," Stanczak said. "There is no great story that goes along with it."

But to me, it really was an interesting story: Sixty-four years ago, that Clipper rolled off the assembly line at the Packard plant just blocks away. Now the

Here is a list of the cars that we saw in Stanczak's two fenced-in lots and his two buildings:

1928 Buick	1952 Studebaker (with two front ends)
1929 Ford Model A Tudor	1953 Buick convertible
1930 Ford Model A	1953 Chevrolet four-door
1930 Ford Model A truck	1955 Oldsmobile
1936 Chevrolet two-door slantback	1956 Ford four-door
1937 Buick four-door	1957 Ford pickup
1937 Packard hot rod	1957 Oldsmobile
1940 Buick four-door	1958 Chevrolet Apache panel truck (2)
1941 Plymouth two-door	1960 Pontiac
1941 Ford Tudor	1964 Cadillac two-door
1947 Chevy coupe	1964 Chevrolet Impala convertible
1947 Plymouth coupe	1964 Dodge Hi-Po sedan
1948 Dodge pickup	1964 Ford Galaxie two-door hardtop
1949 Ford flatbed truck	1964 Pontiac Grand Prix
1949 Chrysler coupe	1965 Buick Wildcat
1949 Cadillac four-door	1965 Chrysler
1950 Ford Tudor	1966 Ford Fairlane
1951 Ford Tudor	1966 Mercury Park Lane
1951 Mercury four-door	1968 Mustang notchback
1951 Chevrolet pickup	1969 Buick Skylark
1951 Buick	1970 Cougar
1952 Oldsmobile coupe (2)	1971 Lincoln Continental MKIII
1952 Packard Clipper	1972 Ford sedan
1952 Ford pickup	Triumph TR7
1952 Ford Victoria	Four Chevrolet Corvairs

A field of dreams? Hardly, but this field next to Stanczak's Quonset hut includes a Valiant, 1952 Olds Rocket 88, Corvair, 1952 Studebaker, and 1941 Plymouth two-door. *Michael Alan Ross*

plant is a disaster with walls and floors falling down, but one of the cars produced there is still in decent, restorable condition less than a mile from where it was born.

I guess they did produce quality products.

"Just ask the man who owns one," as the company's slogan goes.

We had spent much of the day with Stanczak and his terrific granddaughter, Autumn. We were all tired and looking forward to going in separate directions to wash off all the old-car dirt and have a nice meal.

As Michael and I packed up the camera gear in the Woody, Autumn came up to us.

"I really enjoyed being around you guys today."

Not as much as we enjoyed being around you, Autumn.

TOOL TIME
VW REPAIR

The name of the shop is Munk's, and the business is as interesting as the man who owns it.

In my experience, people may become involved in a career because of a passion or hobby, but once they are in that business for a number of years, "the thrill is gone, babe," with all due respect to B. B. King. Being surrounded 24/7 by something you love usually makes you want to go in another direction on nights and weekends—boats, fishing, flying, etc.

But Munk, whose actual name is Chris "Chipmunk" Braden, is stuck in the sixties! When he opened his VW shop in 1969, he was crazy about anything VW: Beetles, Microbuses, Karmann Ghias, dune buggies, etc. Now, nearly a half century later, he is still as crazy about those same cars. I walked though his shop in Waterford, Michigan, and it was like stepping back in time. Here was a split-window VW bus, there was a Corvair-powered dune buggy, with the occasional Porsche 356, 914, or VW Scirocco thrown in for good measure. Oh, and an extremely nice Beck 550 Spyder replica.

Munk's employs a team of mechanics who work in a modern, well-equipped shop. When business is humming, though, sometimes Munk escapes to his secret "man cave," the building where he first opened his VW shop in 1969. It is an old gas station that was originally built in the 1920s. Munk maintains ownership of the building for two reasons: so he doesn't forget where he came from and to have a place to store his private stash of VW restoration projects. "This is one of my buses," he said. "I have three '67s and a '66. I don't fix them up to sell; I fix them because I like them. I have never figured out how to fix up cars to make money."

In another bay of the old building is a Meyers Manx SR2 body that he mounted on a new chassis just the day before. Munk didn't just stumble across a Manx body to restore; he and his brother each bought brand-new Manxes in 1975, and the car he was restoring was his brother's original car. He remembers paying about $2,000 for each kit back then.

When this sign hung over the front door, a young Tim Allen was working as a VW mechanic before starting college and his acting career. At the time, Allen drove a Baja Bug. *Michael Alan Ross*

"The frame rotted away on it, and when he mentioned that he wanted to get the car back together, we installed a brand-new tube frame under the original body," he said. "The quality of the tubes and the welding on this chassis is first class. We are still using the original 1967 transaxle. We'll finish the mechanics and bodywork, install some EMPI wheels, and my brother will take it down to the Florida Keys, where he lives now."

I asked Munk what became of his Manx.

"Oh, I have that in the barn behind the other shop," he said. He mentioned that he hasn't driven it in a number of years and that he should put a little work into it as well.

On the lift next to the Manx is a 1966 VW camper he is in the process of restoring. He explained that nearly every piece of sheet metal is available as a replacement panel these days.

Munk is restoring two VW buses at once. This one, a 1966, was in surprisingly solid condition for a Michigan car. *Michael Alan Ross*

Ugly? Yes. Complete? Yes. Restorable? Maybe. Cheap? Very. At $500, this "runs when parked" Beetle would be an ideal parts car or rat rod. *Michael Alan Ross*

"The inside is still pretty nice," Munk said. "We media blasted the outside, but we'll leave the interior metal alone. My plan is to install a one-fifty-horse-power turbocharged Corvair Spyder engine in this one. I don't need a lot of horsepower; I just need a lot of torque. This will be able to go ninety miles per hour without a problem."

We walked into the yard behind the shop. Munk pointed out his next VW bus project, a 1967 camper. He has owned these VW buses since way before they became valuable.

Next to the camper was a 1966 VW Beetle with the 1,300cc engine. The car was complete but rough.

"I'd take five hundred dollars for that one," he said. I thought that was a decent deal.

"It ran when parked," he said. "It's probably best as a parts car or a rat rod. Speaking of rats, they might be living inside!

"I'm trying to keep all my cars, forever."

I was floored.

"How many do you own?" I asked.

"About seventy," he said. "Just don't tell my wife. My rarest VW is probably the 1954 convertible, a model that they never imported. It was brought to America by someone in the service."

Munk said that as his business has gotten busier and busier, it's become harder to sneak away to work on his own projects.

"It's the only job I've ever had," he said. "But I've had a number of employees work here over the years. One of them was Tim Allen. He came to work here in 1973. It was his first job."

What? You could have knocked me over with a feather. I knew that Allen, the comedian who acted in the television series *Home Improvement*, grew up in Michigan but never knew he had been a mechanic.

"What car did he drive?" I asked.

"I think he built his first car in my shop, a turquoise and white Baja Bug. Even today, he's still a VW guy. I think he has a souped-up Ghia and a souped-up Bug. When he worked here, he wasn't thinking about acting—he was thinking about going to school. So when he left here after the summer, he went to Northern Michigan University. He drove his Baja Bug, but it didn't have a heater, so he was in big trouble in the wintertime."

I mentioned to Munk that my favorite era for modifying cars was in the 1960s, when you could shorten a VW chassis and pop on a fiberglass dune buggy body, install a Corvair engine, and drive it on the beach.

"I'm still living in that era, man," he said.

Lucky guy.

A COLLECTOR WITH A HIGHER CALLING

I was driving down a residential street in the beautiful Boston-Edison neighborhood of Detroit when the shape of a bright red old car caught my attention as we passed a house. I backed up and saw that it was a 1957 Chevy sedan.

When I got the Woody up to the curb, I noticed a couple of other old cars in the driveway. I walked up to the door, rang the doorbell, and then knocked. Nobody answered. So I walked down to the driveway to see the other cars, a couple of older Cadillacs, and a couple of Chevys.

Hmm, nobody home. What to do next? I went to the Woody, got out my notebook and pen, and started to write a note to the owner: Hello, My name is Tom Cotter, and I am writing a book about . . . Just then, a car pulled up to the curb and a man got out.

"Can I help you?" he asked.

"Yes, I'm looking for the owner of these old cars," I said.

"That's me."

Perfect. Just in time.

I showed him the note I had just started, mentioned to him the book we were writing, and asked if he would allow us to interview him and take some photos. No worries. Within just a few minutes, I was to find out that this was one multidimensional fellow.

"My name is Sam White," he said as we started to walk down his driveway collection. "My addiction came from my father. He was big on antique cars. He had a Triumph TR3 that I still own; I just don't have here right now."

He said his father bought the Triumph in 1977. Today, he keeps it in another storage facility.

"He also had a Jaguar," White said. "But the cars in my driveway are my addiction. I've had that 1956 Cadillac since my kids were young, probably ten or fifteen years."

As we toured the cars in White's driveway, I noticed Harvard University decals on the back windows of several cars.

"What's with the Harvard stickers?" I asked. "Did you go there?"

"Yes, I graduated from the Harvard Divinity School," he said. "It's where I got my masters in theological study in 1988."

"You mean you are a minister?"

"Yes. Well, actually my title is Reverend Doctor Samuel White III."

The 1957 Chevy that caught my attention as we were driving through the Boston-Edison neighborhood. That red car led to a discovery of a bunch of other cool cars. *Michael Alan Ross*

Suddenly, I was intimidated. I'd never been confronted before by a car guy who was also a minister and a doctor.

Reverend White has been pastor of the Friendship Baptist Church in Detroit for twenty years. His family has lived in this house, which was built in 1916, for twenty-two.

Anyway, we continued our tour of his collection.

"I bought that Caddy from a guy in Detroit for four hundred or five hundred dollars," he said. "It runs, but they all need work."

"Then there is the '46 Cadillac four-door that I got from a friend. That car runs better than any car I own. It's a straight eight. I bought it from another pastor who worked on old cars too. I paid like twenty-five hundred dollars, and the engine just hums."

We worked our way toward cars on the side of the driveway.

One car was covered, but I felt through the cover and identified it as a 1956 Chevy.

"And the other car is a 1951 Chevy," he said. "I need to get rid of both those cars. I got them for little or next to nothing. But I've got to get some cars out of here."

The 1956 Chevy is a four-door sedan. It is rough but very complete with a six-cylinder.

"I'd like to get a couple of grand for that one," he said. "The 1951 apparently runs as well, although I've never heard it. I'd like to get a grand for that. I'm just trying to clean out my driveway."

The car White drives most is the 1957 Chevy. It's not for sale.

"I'd probably sell that '56 Caddy too. It's a four-door hardtop and runs well. I'd like five thousand dollars for that one."

Next, he said something that really got me stoked.

"I want you to stand next to the garage door, and I'm going to go into the house and open it up," White said. "I think you'll like what's inside."

So Michael and I waited in the driveway as White disappeared into the house for a couple of minutes. Then the huge carriage house doors started to open. I saw pink. Big and pink.

It was a pink 1959 Cadillac. Huge! Elvis style.

The Caddy was impressive enough, but it was the two cars behind it that almost brought me to tears.

Jags.

Two of them.

Now, full disclosure: I've never told this to anyone, but I'll share my fantasy with you. It goes like this: Every time I open a garage or barn door that has been closed for a long time, I imagine a Jaguar XK120 or XK140 inside waiting to be discovered. Not a Chevy or even an MG, but a Jaguar. After more than half a century of opening doors, I have found many Model As, old Plymouths, and John Deere tractors, but never a Jag. Until this moment.

The Reverend Dr. Samuel White III had not one but two Jaguar XK140s sitting next to the pink Cadillac, a coupe and a roadster.

A crowded and interesting collection! Reverend White bought the 1959 Cadillac when he was shopping for a Mother's Day gift. "Was your wife pleased?" *Michael Alan Ross*

The reverend actually enjoys driving this XK140 fixed-head coupe more than the roadster because the hardtop adds structural rigidity to the body. *Michael Alan Ross*

But let's talk about the Cadillac first.

"I went out to get a Mother's Day gift, but on the way there, I saw these fins," he said. "I said, 'Oh my God, I have to go see that.' Well . . . I bought it and drove it home from 14 Mile." Happy Mother's Day! "It ran well except for the brakes."

The Reverend Doctor Samuel White III must be married to a saint to accept a pink Caddy for Mother's Day! OK, on to the Jags. I gave the good reverend my business card and told him that when he needs money to send his kids to college, he should call me. That I would be a customer of that 1955 XK140 roadster.

"OK, that car is Tom's," he said.

He actually enjoys the Jaguar fixed-head coupe more than the roadster.

"There was a place called Frog Motors in Detroit, and they worked on nothing but foreign cars," White said.

"They were going out of business, so they sold me these cars, one for three thousand dollars and the other for five thousand dollars. I got them dirt cheap."

He bought both cars about ten or fifteen years ago. What a deal.

"Everything works, the engine, the brakes," he said. "The roadster just needs new paint."

He bought the 1957 black coupe at the same time.

"Deal of a lifetime," he admitted.

Reverend White had the brick garage set up like a sports car shop in England: flags, banners, and signs were draped on the walls around the two cars. The garage was packed with the Caddy and the two Jags. Then their owner told us that he usually packs his father's old TR3 Triumph in here as well, between the Jaguars.

This guy was a space-efficiency expert. I asked him which car he enjoyed driving the most.

"Well, it would be the Triumph because it was my dad's," he said. "It's the car I would get rid of last. I was offered fifteen thousand for the car, but that was Dad's; I can't sell Dad's car. Every Father's Day, I get that car out and I drive it."

Reverend White's father is deceased, but you can tell his son still misses him.

"My father was one of the first African American corporate executives for Xerox," he said. "We lived in Rochester, New York. He died at forty-nine years old."

This 1956 Cadillac runs well, yet Reverend White wants to reduce his "cylinder count," so he will likely sell it. *Michael Alan Ross*

So seeing one red Chevy in a driveway had led us to meet one of the coolest collectors in Detroit, a man whose eclectic garage included three Cadillacs, three Chevys, two Jaguars, and one Triumph TR3. I asked Reverend White if either of his kids shared his passion for cars.

"I told my son, 'That '57 Chevy is yours. Let's work on it.' But he didn't really care. Unfortunately that is a typical reaction for that generation."

We discussed the challenge of keeping old cars running.

"I must admit, this is a rich man's hobby," he said. "I bought them all cheap and do a little bit at a time. But I do enjoy it."

ELLA'S LINCOLN AND SUPPORTING CAST

Before even opening the gates, Steve Amiot said we could expect a spectacular sunset and lighting on the mountains behind us.

"See those mountains over there?" he asked.

"Those are called the Sandias, which in Spanish means 'watermelon.' In the evening, they turn pink, like watermelon." Photographers Michael Alan Ross, Jordon Lewis, and Ben Woodsworth were excited to hear that.

I asked why he had so many cars. "I'm a car guy," he said. "I'm supposed to be retired from the restaurant business, but I've been doing this car stuff full time for thirty-five years. These cars are the result.

"My wife says to get rid of them and let's go on a vacation, but I can't agree with her, you know?"

I sure do. We started at one end of his yard and progressed to the other, talking as we went. We walked past an old Ford truck. I asked why the fender had been widened. "It's a '51, and it's been converted to a dually," he said. "It was a farm truck used in the southeast corner of the state. The flathead engine runs well and only needs a water pump. I call it yard art; it belongs to a friend who never intends to sell it, so it just sits in my yard."

He walked us toward his shop, where he polishes and removes dents from stainless-steel automobile trim as a side business. He also rents one garage bay to a friend who paints cars. He showed us his 1958 Chevy four-door station wagon, one of two he has. "This one is a Yeoman, one of the rarest Chevys there is," he said. "These are usually powered by six-cylinders, but this one has a two eighty-three

One of two 1958 Chevy station wagons Steve Amiot has in his collection. The other is a restored A/C-equipped car. The good news is that just about everything he has is for sale at reasonable prices. *Michael Alan Ross*

and some rare options: power brakes, super rare; power steering, super rare; factory air conditioning, super, super rare on the cheapest wagon Chevy made in 1958. This one is definitely for sale, probably in the twenty thousands." Amiot also showed us a replica he is building of the first 1968 COPO big-block Camaro. "Don Yenko built all his 1968 Camaros from Super Sport models, but he ordered one standard model from Chevrolet with a Corvette engine installed from the factory," he said. "So this is a copy of that car."

Amiot told us about a friend in a nearby valley along the river who has two hundred cars in his yard, mostly from the thirties, forties, fifties, and a few from the sixties.

"He had this old Lincoln sitting in the corner, so I approached him one day and said, 'That's a pretty straight '61 Lincoln.' He said, 'Yeah, would you believe that it used to belong to jazz singer Ella Fitzgerald?'

"I said, 'No, actually I don't believe it, but it's a good story.'" Amiot said about seventy of his friend's cars were towed away when he failed to comply with the county's old car ordinance. "I had already bought two solid Buick Rivieras from him, a 1963 and a 1964," Amiot said. "Well, after so many of his cars were repossessed, he called and said he would like to have those Rivieras back.

"He said, 'Come on down here and see what else you want, and I'll trade for those Rivieras.'"

So Amiot went to his friend's house in the valley and clamped his eyes on a 1948 Chrysler coupe. Then he saw that Lincoln again. "I asked if he had any

Of course, the prize of Amiot's yard was this 1961 Lincoln Continental, bought new by jazz singer Ella Fitzgerald. The car is straight and solid and would be the ideal collector car for a jazz enthusiast. *Michael Alan Ross*

Of course, as soon as Brian heard that the Lincoln was owned by a celebrity, he had to get involved. Here he is sitting in the right rear seat, exactly where Ella sat when she was chauffeured around Beverly Hills. *Michael Alan Ross*

proof that this was Ella's car," he said. "He said, 'Yeah, I think so.' So a week later, he showed me the original registration from the 1960s."

Amiot showed me the registration, which matched the original California black license plate. "So I thought that was cool, and I traded," he said. He told me to look at the back seat. "She would always sit in the right side in the back seat," he said. "Her driver would sit in the front. She never drove the car; she would only tour and sing. She had a mansion in Beverly Hills.

"When she would go to the Copa Cabana or *The Tonight Show*, she would always sit on curbside so she could make the grand entrance. So the back seat has an indentation where she always sat." The car only has seventy-six thousand miles on it.

"She lived in Europe a lot, so this car was not used too much," he said. "She would perform with Dizzy Gillespie and Louis Armstrong. Tony Bennett recently said that Ella Fitzgerald was the greatest singer he ever heard."

I asked him why he kept the windows open. He said because he didn't want condensation to develop (and because the electric windows are broken).

"We don't have much rain around here anyway," he said. Amiot said he would sell Ella's Lincoln for $5,000. I think that is a steal.

Next, we moved on to the rest of his yard. A 1964 Ford Galaxie convertible was next to a Falcon Futura Sprint with a V-8 and four-speed.

"It's another one of those cars I'll probably never get to," Amiot said of the Falcon. In another spot was a Studebaker Lark station wagon and a 1958 Pontiac. It was a barn finder's dream. "That Pontiac is an original Santa Cruz car," he said. "I'd let that go for a grand. And the Lark is a Daytona model, which means that in 1963, it had an R2 V-8 motor and disc brakes.

"And it has the mechanical sliding rear roof."

We walked into his other yard. I was in front with Amiot while Brian, Michael, Clair, Jordon, and Ben followed with their various cameras. I kept warning them to watch out for the "landmines" that were left by Amiot's large but friendly dog.

Barn-finding, after all, is not for clean freaks. Amiot showed us a 1969 Chevelle that he would sell for $1,500. Then we came upon another car that got my attention—a 1954 Ford two-door Ranch Wagon. I explained to him that I still own a 1953 Ranch Wagon that I bought as a senior in high school. "This belonged to a guy who had a tow truck," he said. "He hauled cars he found along Route 66. When he died, he had some beauties, but this one became surplus. I'll take four hundred dollars for the whole car."

I noticed it had the "Ranch Wagon" emblems I have been searching for. I offered him $100 for the logos, but he said he would only sell the whole car, not just the emblems. (At press time of *Route 66 Barn Find Road Trip*, I was still trying to convince him to sell me the emblems . . .)

We came across a Saab Sonnet—the more angular, second-generation model.

"I drove that car eighty-five miles per hour," he said. "Paid five hundred dollars for it. But then the master cylinder went out, so I just parked it."

The correct V-4 Ford industrial engine powered it, and it had a four-speed on the column and correct alloy rims with red-striped tires. This one had a customized front end, so the headlights had been lowered into the grille. Still, it was a rare fiberglass sports car for sale for just $1,500. I said I would take it if he would deliver it to my home in North Carolina. He said his nephew lives in Mooresville, just one town away from mine. I encouraged him to visit his nephew and bring the car to me.

Ben, from Hagerty, said that his first car was a 1974 Sonnet. Small world. There were more vehicles—Lincolns, Mustangs, an interesting '66 Chevy pickup with a built-on camper. There were other '58 Chevys, a four-door hardtop, a '58 Biscayne two-door sedan, and another Studebaker Lark. This was a worthwhile stop. We thanked Amiot, but before we left, Jordon and Ben asked if they could stay until after sunset in order to capture the amazing lighting against the pink mountains.

Before we left Amiot's, he showed us some concrete pavement on the rear of his property along the railroad tracks. "This was part of the original Route 66 from before World War II," he said. "I had to dig up a lot of it when I built these buildings and to run water and electrical lines underground. It's at least twelve inches thick."

What that meant was that the last couple of hours we had spent looking at old cars had been not near, but literally on the original Route 66. Amiot suggested that before we leave town, we should visit Silva's Saloon, the oldest bar in New Mexico. How could we decline? Silva's was opened in 1933 after Prohibition ended. Felix Silva Sr. owned it, and today his son, Felix Silva Jr., runs it. It has been featured in numerous magazine stories, TV documentaries, and movies.

"I've been coming here since I was six months old," said Felix Jr. "People have been just leaving stuff here from the beginning," which explains the huge amount of paraphernalia on the walls. Felix Jr. said that the bar was selected by *Esquire* magazine in 2000 as one of the top five bars in America. So, while we waited for Jordon and Ben to finish up their sunset video project, we enjoyed a couple of beers. It was a great way to end the day.

INDEX